Richard Roos, S.J.

Christwalk

Paulist Press New York/Mahwah

Acknowledgement

Quotations from the *Revised Standard Version of the Bible,* copyrighted 1946, 1952 © 1971, 1973, by the National Council of Churches of Christ in the U.S.A. are reprinted by permission. Excerpts from the *New American Bible,* copyright © 1970 by the Confraternity of Christian Doctrine, Washington, D.C., are used by permission of the copyright holder. All rights reserved. The lyrics of *Be Not Afraid* by Robert J. Dufford, S.J. copyright © 1975 by Robert J. Dufford, S.J. and North American Liturgy Resources, 10802 North 23rd Avenue, Phoenix, Ariz. 85029, are used with permission. All rights reserved. The lyrics of *Only in God* by John B. Foley, S.J., copyright © 1976 by John B. Foley, S.J. and North American Liturgy Resources, are used with permission. All rights reserved. Lyrics from *To Be Your Body* by Joe Wise are used by permission of G.I.A. Publications, Chicago. The quotation by Pedro Arrupe, S.J. is reprinted by permission of The Institute of Jesuit Sources.

Maps by Frank Sabatté, C.S.P.

Cover design by Pedro Carrasquillo, S.J.

Library of Congress
Catalog Card Number: 84-61491

ISBN: 0-8091-2667-2 (Paper) 0-8091-0374-5 (Cloth)

Published by Paulist Press
997 Macarthur Boulevard
Mahwah, New Jersey 07430

Printed and bound in the
United States of America

Contents

Prologue

"Leave Your Home"
Gen 12:1

At some moment in our development many of us experience an urge to ritualize in a radical way the values that underpin our lives. If we yield to that urge, it can lead us to freedoms we never imagined. In March of 1979 I left home for six weeks to become a pilgrim—walking, praying, and begging. For the eight hundred miles of the old California Mission Trail I ate what people gave me and slept where they took me in. More importantly I came to know the Lord, myself, and other people in ways that would have otherwise been impossible. This book is the account of my outer and inner journey.

Historically, pilgrimages were journeys to holy places undertaken for religious reasons. They were common to all the great religions of the world, both before and after the advent of Christianity. Ancient Egyptians and Babylonians traveled to sacred tombs and shrines to offer sacrifice. The pilgrimage to Mecca is still one of the pillars of Islam. And in our own tradition the history of Israel is punctuated by holy migrations, originating with Abraham's call to "Go forth from the land of your kinsfolk and from your father's house to a land that I will show you . . . and I will bless you" (Gen 12:1–3). Out of Abraham's obedience was born the covenant. The exodus from Egypt, with its ensuing forty-year pilgrimage, is the watershed of Israelite history and worship.

In the New Testament Jesus is depicted as the ultimate pilgrim, leaving the homeland of divinity to trudge through the deserts of humanity. He was frequently on the road: fleeing to Egypt as an infant; visiting Jerusalem at twelve; praying in the desert after his baptism; wandering through Galilee, Judea, Samaria, and the Decapolis to preach the Kingdom. He lived on the margin of society, though always in touch with the people.

Christianity became a world religion, and Christian pilgrimage developed into a popular ascetical and devotional practice in imitation of Jesus. Throughout Christian history pilgrims have been living symbols of the Church. From its infancy the Church has called itself "the pilgrim people of God," on the move toward eternity. Christian art and liturgy abound with images and references to pilgrimage.

In medieval Europe Christian pilgrimage became an institution. Large bands of pilgrims put on penitential beggars' garb and trekked to some distant cathedral or martyr's tomb to win pardon and absolution of sins. They went with the bishop's blessing and letters of safe conduct. Special roads and hostels were built to accommodate them. Set rituals marked their visit, such as all-night vigils, monetary gifts to the shrine, leaving some relic of a cure (e.g., crutches), reception of the sacraments of reconciliation and Eucharist (rare in those days), and long hours of prayer on their knees.

Since methods of travel were slow and arduous, pilgrimages tended to be long, difficult, and dangerous. The threat of shipwreck or robbery was much more real than it is today. Consequently the reasons that compelled people to set out had to be serious. Pilgrims traveled to holy places to get something they greatly wanted or needed: the granting of some divine favor, such as physical, mental, or spiritual healing; forgiveness of some grave sin through prayer and penance; or just peace of soul in time of turmoil. Often they went to thank God for some large favor already received. These motives drew tens of thousands of Christians to leave their homes and loved ones for weeks, months, or even years.

In the sixteenth century, one of these pilgrims was Ignatius Loyola, the founder of the Jesuits. After his conversion from nominal, late-medieval Catholicism, Inigo set aside his wealth and vanity to follow God. He donned the robe of a beggar, lived on alms, and walked around healing souls through spiritual conversation.

When he founded the Society of Jesus, Ignatius tried to instill in the novices his own detachment from material goods and his own desire to imitate Christ in poverty, humility, and mobility. In addition to directing them through the thirty-day Spiritual Exercises, he would send novices out for a month of pilgrimage. They were to take no money or food, but were to simply walk, pray, and beg for whatever they needed along the way. If they came back after a month and still wanted to be Jesuits, they could continue their novitiate, provided they brought letters from people they had visited testifying to the worthiness of their conduct.

Eighteenth and nineteenth century eastern Europe, and especially Russia, saw the emergence of perpetual pilgrims, like the anonymous author of the classic *The Way of the Pilgrim*.[1] These "fools for Christ" would spend their whole lives walking from shrine to shrine, begging, praying, and preaching the word of the Lord from the wisdom of their hearts.

In the contemporary world, as in the past, the pilgrim is a marginal person. The pilgrim moves along the fringes of society, not settling at a distance like the hermit, but weaving daily in and out among the lives of ordinary people. What marginalizes the pilgrim is his or her freedom from all that establishes people in society: home, family, roots and personal history, political and religious community, job and economic solvency.

On the other hand, the pilgrim is dependent on society for sustenance, shelter, and even affirmation. Unlike the hermit, the pilgrim's need and desire for society gives public witness to all that is genuine and life-giving in society. Hence the pilgrim is attractive to people in the mainstream, affirming their goodness and showing them a freedom they quietly envy.

At the same time, the pilgrim's freedom challenges the compromising and dehumanizing effects of conventional living. It silently rebukes the cultural values and social mores that clog people's ideals. If he or she serves effectively, the pilgrim causes the structured community to rediscover itself, renewing the vitality with which it can voice its own vision and *raison d'être*. "I have come not to abolish the law," said Jesus, "but to fulfill it." The true pilgrim calls the old and traditional back to its pristine relevance.

My pilgrimage of the California missions did a little bit of that in a few people's lives. There were no bold miracles, but there were a number of humble ones. Again and again I saw grace dissolve the natural human tendencies toward suspicion, distrust, and alienation. Very ordinary people opened their homes to a total stranger, simply because he asked for food and lodging in the name of the Lord. They risked. I pray they will be rewarded.

My purpose in writing this account is not simply expository. I hope it will be for the reader a reflection on his or her own pilgrimage from conception to resurrection. I hope also that it will point out the value of pilgrimage as an ascetical and apostolic exercise even in modern times. Perhaps through *Christwalk* others will feel called to "leave home," either literally or metaphorically, so that Christianity will continue to be challenged into vitality.

Christwalk is dedicated to all those who welcomed me along the way. Their courage, their kindness, and their belief in the goodness of the human spirit taught me more about Christ than I ever learned from a book.

Preparation

"Neither Gold Nor Silver"
Mt 10:9

Preparation for my pilgrimage began sixteen years earlier. While in the Jesuit novitiate I read about St. Ignatius sending his novices out as pilgrims. I was eighteen and full of enthusiasm, and the romance of wandering around penniless for Christ was attractive. I wanted to do something outstanding for the Lord—something heroic. But the focus was more on my doing it than on the Lord's wanting it. My motives were sincere but immature. Ignatius tells of the same kind of desires in the early days of his own conversion. It is hard to accept that the most heroic sanctity is often achieved in doing ordinary tasks well. My master of novices explained to me why the pilgrimage had been dropped from modern Jesuit formation. Times had changed and society was much less tolerant of strangers, beggars, and Christians. I nodded, but was quietly disappointed.

All through the years of my Jesuit training I was taught that the ideal for the Jesuit was to imitate Christ in real poverty and humiliations. We were called to be like him because of our love for him, and we were called to be counter-cultural signs to the world. I kept chafing at the bit, wanting to do something concrete. My desire to make a pilgrimage never completely died, but I resigned myself to its impracticality. Some years later the hope was enlivened when I heard of two instances of American Jesuits making modified pilgrimages. I still put the thought aside, lacking a suitable shrine to visit and lacking the freedom to just take a couple of months off. I had also matured to the point where I realized that the only worthwhile acts of devotion are the ones that God calls us to. And I had accepted the fact that God was not calling me to be a pilgrim.

Then everything changed. I had been ordained a priest and had spent four years as a high school chaplain and religion teacher. In August 1978, at the age of thirty-four, I began tertianship. This final phase of spiritual training comes after many years of study and a few years of active ministry. Its goal is to integrate the academic and pastoral with the Jesuit's relationship to God in prayer. Some call it "the school of the heart." During tertianship the Jesuit experiences the thirty-day retreat for the second time, studies the history and constitutions of the Order, and enjoys the leisure necessary for reflection and inner growth. It is perhaps the last time he will have the luxury of such an extended period of freedom from the regular grind.

Since we New Englanders have the reputation of being unable to conceive of anything west of the Hudson River, I thought it would be good to go to California for tertianship. An excellent nine-month program had been started in Berkeley in connection with the Jesuit School of Theology there. The director was Fr. Edward Malatesta, who had taught at the Gregorian University in Rome. We were nine in the community: Ed, his assistant Bernie Carroll from Canada, and seven tertians.

My first important experience of the tertianship was the Long Retreat at the Jesuit novitiate in Montecito, just outside Santa Barbara. On a "break day" near the end of the retreat, a Jesuit from a local parish gave me a tour of Old Mission Santa Barbara and the Historical Society. In the museum was a map of the twenty-one Franciscan missions of California, forming a chain from San Diego to Sonoma, forty miles north of San Francisco. I had heard of the old Spanish missions, but until that day I had been

10

unaware that they were so numerous and that they had formed the major north-south travel route in the late eighteenth and early nineteenth centuries. In the course of his explanation, my friend said, "They're supposed to be a day's walk apart." Instantly the word "pilgrimage" came into my head. For the next two days I was obsessed with the desire to walk the missions in the steps of Fr. Junipero Serra, the great apostle of California who started founding the missions in 1769. Visions of imitating Christ in radical dependence on the Father crowded all other thoughts out of my prayer. I lost all peace of soul. Though I felt I should be praying about the matter of the retreat, I could concentrate only on walking the missions.

When I told my director about these "distractions," he asked, "Why do you call them distractions? Maybe they're really from the Lord. Why don't you accept them and discern them? See if it's really what the Lord is calling you to." Ed had a way of making things sound simple.

It was very important to me to be as certain as possible that a pilgrimage, if I made one, was really a call from the Lord. I suspected that there would be times on the road when that conviction would be my only reason for not giving up. Therefore I embarked on a discernment process, weighing the pros and cons, and observing my spiritual consolations and desolations. Over and over the signals grew clearer. Everything said, "Go."

I sent a detailed proposal to my Provincial in Boston, outlining my reasons for wanting to go. He had a right to approve or veto my foolishness. In the proposal I assured him that I would undergo a complete physical exam to verify that my health was adequate for such an undertaking. I also specified a number of safety precautions. I would walk during daylight only, seeking shelter an hour before sunset. I would not hitchhike or accept rides, except in an emergency. My route would avoid freeways, where walking was illegal and dangerous. I would carry a couple of dimes for emergency phone calls, and I would phone the tertians regularly to assure them of my safety. I would be on pilgrimage for the season of Lent, leaving the day after Ash Wednesday and returning to the community by Easter. If I were still on the road on Holy Saturday, the tertians would pick me up wherever I was and drive me home. With those provisions, the Provincial readily granted permission.

The question arose about whether I would identify myself as a priest. I decided not to. Clericalism has hurt the Church too seriously in the past, and still does. I judged that it would be wise not to use my status as a cleric to win acceptance. I wanted to be met as *who* I was, not as *what* I was. If people invited me into their homes merely as a Christian pilgrim, I would then, upon further questioning, be completely open about my identity. The one exception to this rule would be rectories. They get many freeloaders and con artists. It would be only fair to let them know from the start that I was a Jesuit—though telling them *that* might be a liability!

After receiving the Provincial's permission, I began to acquire what I needed to take with me. Since I would be begging food and lodging, camping equipment would be unnecessary. I wanted to be as spartan as possible, without being foolhardy. Jesus had said to the Twelve when he sent them on mission, "Provide yourselves with neither gold nor silver nor copper in your belts; no traveling bag, no change of shirt, no sandals, no walking staff." I did not feel called to go that far. Partly out of pride, however, and partly out of devotion (an old-fashioned word that I am not completely comfortable with, but cannot improve on), I did want to imitate the apostles' austerity and dependence on the Father's care. I decided to take a small backpack with a change of clothes and whatever else would be reasonable. I would carry a sturdy, but light staff. It eventually became more useful than I could have foreseen. Without it I would not have persevered.

Suitable hiking boots would be a priority. Never having owned a pair, I did not know what to look for. By nature I am not the athletic type. At a sporting goods store in Berkeley I found a gray-haired salesman who was an experienced hiker. After two or three well-framed questions he deduced that I was "doing the mission trail." He took me under his wing and gave me abundant advice about boots, socks, heel cushions, and even methods of walking. At the end of my journey the boots he sold me still had plenty of rubber on them.

Over the next two months I gradually collected necessities for the trip: backpack, clothing, a compact Bible (Old and New Testaments) that I could get into the hip pocket of my jeans, journal books, snakebite kit, plastic poncho, travel toothbrush, route maps, needle and thread, etc. I was surprised at how many incidentals were required by prudence for a journey on which I was taking almost nothing. My full pack weighed about fifteen pounds.

Partly because of the weight, but mostly because of the nature of pilgrimage, I did not carry a camera. That was a difficult decision because I like to photograph places I visit. I realized, however, that if I had a camera with me there was danger that I would slip into being more of a tourist than a pilgrim. I have many memories now, but no pictures.

The day before I left, I decided not to take a wristwatch. One of my neuroses was a compulsion about time. I was a watchoholic. I decided that this would be a good occasion to be free of that. There would be no need to know the time, so why bother? It was a good decision. Even without a watch I had more than enough indications of time along the way, such as clocks in stores, gas stations, and people's homes.

The months leading up to my departure were a patchwork of conflicting feelings of eagerness and trepidation. There were times I cringed at the prospect of being

13

laughed at and having doors slammed in my face. I even fantasized getting arrested for vagrancy. That fear served a good purpose. It convinced me to carry two or three pieces of identification.

Once while in a period of doubt, I did something completely out of character. I opened the Bible to see if what I read would give me any clarity. The first words my eyes fell on were from Acts 9:15-16, in which the Lord encourages the Christian Ananias not to fear the persecutor Saul, who has been recently converted:

> But the Lord said to him, "Go, for he is a chosen instrument of mine to carry my name before the Gentiles and kings and the children of Israel; for I will show him how much he must suffer for the sake of my name." (RSV) [2]

Despite the reference to suffering, the passage shored up my sagging resolve.

Another Scripture gave me strength for the journey, too. I was celebrating Eucharist with the tertianship community two days before leaving. My homily was going to be a short expression of what it meant to me to be finally on my way after all the months of anticipation. Again unlike my usual behavior, I had not looked at the readings before Mass. When I came to read the Gospel, it happened to be these verses from the tenth chapter of Mark:

> Peter was moved to say to Jesus, "We have put aside everything to follow you!" Jesus answered, "I give you my word, there is no one who has given up home, brothers or sisters, mother or father, children or property, for me and for the gospel who will not receive in this present age a hundred times as many homes, brothers and sisters, mothers, children and property—and persecution besides—and in the age to come everlasting life." (NAB)

14

That text became a companion to me during the next six weeks. In my homily that evening I think I finally put into words, even to my own satisfaction, why I was going on pilgrimage. All of the reasons based on Jesuit tradition or Christian witness were overshadowed by the one compelling belief that it was the Lord's will for me. It was a call that I had to answer in order to be truly myself. Had there been no other reason, that would have been enough. Sometimes it seems too simple, but it is the fact: I went because I had to.

I

"I Will Speak to Your Heart"
Hos 2:16

San Diego to Montecito
March 1–15, 1979

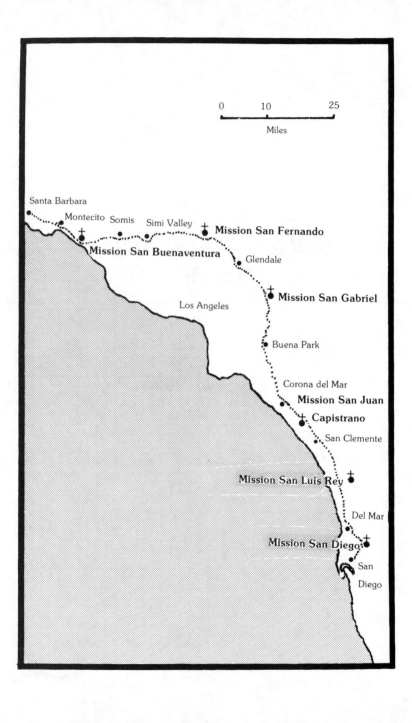

Thursday, March 1.

The first day was not exactly what I had envisioned. It rained. I had chosen to start from the south to avoid that. Wasn't there a song about it never raining in Southern California? The sun had been out in Oakland when my plane took off, but here in San Diego it was pouring. After waiting for it to let up somewhat, I spent much of the eleven miles between the airport and the old mission clutching my hooded poncho close to my chin and skirting or sloshing through puddles wider than the road.

The ninety-minute flight had been a jumble of feelings: eagerness to begin; fear of failure; hope for personal growth and deepening intimacy with God; sadness at leaving my community in Berkeley; insecurity about being actually poor and having to beg; excitement at the adventure of it all; and embarrassment at embarking on something so foolish. Once airborne I was committed to either finishing at Easter or quitting along the way. The former would be trying, the latter humiliating—and I did not know which would be worse. Either way, I was scared.

About halfway to the mission the rain eased off even more, and prayer became easier. I was using the Jesus Prayer. It has many variations, my favorite being, "Lord Jesus Christ, Son of the living God, have mercy on me, a sinner." At different times I would abbreviate it, e.g., "Jesus, have mercy," "Son of God, mercy," or simply,

"Jesus." Slowly, repeatedly, I murmured it. Slowly, deeply, it seeped into my mind, soul, and footsteps, distracting me from my fears. It became a mantra for centering, even while stumping through city streets. My pace fell into rhythm with the prayer. I found I could almost forget the rain and the traffic. Like the author of *The Way of the Pilgrim,* I could engage in peaceful union with God while walking, a kind of prayer better suited to pilgrimage than the Ignatian meditation and contemplation I had learned during my Jesuit training. Just as the stillness of the body enables the movement of reason and imagination in the Ignation Spiritual Exercises, I discovered that the stillness of the mind in the Jesus Prayer allowed my body to move along without loss of recollection. I soon abandoned my plan of spending an hour each day in meditation, favoring instead the Jesus Prayer. That was a mistake. It caused me to lose sight of the value of stasis as a counterbalance to movement. A fundamental end of pilgrimage is attainment of the inner freedom to follow the most subtle urgings of the Spirit, along with the sensitivity to notice those urgings. Such freedom and sensitivity are nurtured by contemplative stillness. In denying myself those times of quiet meditation I not only limited the ways in which the Lord could touch me, but I also unduly exalted movement. As the miles went by, walking became less a way of meeting God and more a means of making progress toward a goal. Ironically my chief struggle during the pilgrimage was against the temptation to absolutize the value of progress.

I darkened the door of Mission San Diego de Alcala at about 3:15, wet from a final downpour, and asked to see the Friar in charge. I still thought the missions were maintained by Franciscans. Only five are, San Diego not being one of them. It is a parish run by diocesan priests.

I was sent from the gift shop to the parish office, and from there to the rectory. A gaunt, kindly priest with thinning grey hair greeted me and led me to a small office. I told my story and asked if I could celebrate Mass and stay the night. He said he would have to ask the monsignor. There was an awkward silence as he studied my dripping poncho, backpack, stick, and boots. He seemed to want to let me stay, but suspected there would be a problem. Then he left me alone while he consulted the pastor. Returning after several minutes, the priest probed with more questions. I offered my identification papers and he disappeared again to show these to the monsignor. I felt like the cowardly lion at the gate of Oz.

Coming back the second time, the priest told me that the monsignor wanted to speak with me. At last I was going to meet him, I thought. No, not yet. The associate picked up a nearby phone and handed me the receiver. The pastor was on the line. I explained my pilgrimage briefly to him and repeated my requests. The monsignor (I had not yet been told his name) sounded cordial but non-committal. I was welcome to concelebrate at the 5:30 Mass in the church with the assistant, but there would be no room for me in the rectory that night. And I should be forewarned not to expect to be taken in on such short notice at the other missions, either.

I hung up the phone, not fully believing what was happening. I began to feel empty. My heroic beginnings lay limp at my feet. Turned away from the very first mission! How could this happen? How would I be able to beg a place to stay in the rain? I had never begged lodging before. I felt confused, afraid, and angry. It wasn't at all the way I had planned it.

I told the assistant I would go to the church and pray for a place to spend the night. He looked concerned, but helpless. As I was leaving he revealed that my staff reminded him of John the Baptist. Encouraged by his gentleness, I asked if I could have some food after Mass. He assured me that I would be taken care of.

In church I felt dejected and fearful. "The foxes have lairs, the birds in the sky have nests, but the Son of Man

21

has nowhere to lay his head" (Mt 8:20). I knew what Jesus meant. Then I remembered another verse: "Consider the ravens: they do not sow, they do not reap, they have neither cellar nor barn—yet God feeds them. How much more important you are than the birds!" (Lk 12:24–25). Why worry? God will take care of me as he cares for the birds. Next I began to have feelings of anger toward the monsignor. It was hard to fight them off. He was only doing what he thought was right. I had come crashing into his world unexpectedly and he had no room for me. I began to pray for him.

After a while my self-possession returned enough for me to notice that the church was cold and damp. The high ceiling and bare stone floor did not help. Sitting still made me feel chilled, so I toured the mission garden and museum, returning to the church in time for Mass. My jeans were still damp and muddy, so I declined the invitation to concelebrate. Before the liturgy started, I sat shivering and in poor spirits. I was angry at God. Yet during Mass, I was moved by warm feelings of intimacy with him. Things were bad, but I clung to a belief that they would improve.

I went to the sacristy after Mass to see about getting some food. At that point my situation began to change. The associate handed me a small brown envelope and asked me to offer Mass for a particular intention along my way. The envelope contained a five dollar bill.

Then the priest introduced me to the sacristan, Lily, a white-haired grandmother and retired teacher who served as the C.C.D. coordinator for the parish. Apparently he had told her about me.

"Where are you going from here, Father?" she asked.

"Well, I'm going to the rectory for something to eat. But then I'm not sure. They have no room for me there, and I don't know anyone in the area, so I guess I'll have to go begging." I had already begun.

"Oh, that's too bad, Father. I'd put you up myself, but I don't have a spare room. All I have is a fold-out sofa bed in the living room. I'd offer it to you if I thought you'd take it."

"Really?" My eyes widened. I wasted no time in accepting the offer, which I suspect had been orchestrated by the assistant pastor. Lily said she would pick me up after dinner.

That was the turning point. On just the first day I had experienced a little death and resurrection. Now everything was different. I felt safe again.

The assistant took me to a nicely appointed dining room where, at last, I met the pastor, whose manner was warmer and more hospitable than before. He was chancellor of the diocese, and a professor at the University of San Diego. He appeared to be in his late forties, though his hair was white. I was seated with my back to a blazing hearth, and together the three of us made short work of an ample pork chop dinner. The monsignor seemed genuinely interested in my pilgrimage. He asked many questions, nodding understanding and approval. By the end of the meal, he offered to phone ahead to the next couple of missions to make sure I was given hospitality. When I declined the courtesy, he was gracious, but a little mystified. I was tempted to let him call, but I knew that would be feathering my nest a little too cozily.

Lily appeared shortly after 7:00. We stopped at a supermarket, where she proceeded to buy food for my lunch the next day—and the next, and the one after that. She was a practiced grandmother, buying enough to last me till Easter. When I left in the morning, I took only half of what she wanted to give me, and I still had trouble fitting it all into my pack.

At her apartment we talked about her teaching, past and present, and about her children and grandchildren. We looked at my maps together and tried to figure out the best route toward Mission San Luis Rey. I decided I would shoot for Del Mar the next day, about halfway to the mission. The monsignor had told me about a parish there, where I could stay if I could not find other lodging. Lily directed me along some back roads that were not on my maps. She also gave me a detailed map of the L.A. area, much clearer than my own.

As I dropped off to sleep, I thanked God for the warmth and dryness of a bed, a gift I usually take for granted.

Friday, March 2.

Lily and I went to the mission for the 7:00 A.M. Mass, which I concelebrated with the monsignor. The custom, dating back to Father Serra's time, is to ring the mission bells before Mass. At 6:59 a tiny altar boy in cassock and surplice climbed the stone steps from the garden to the back of the bell wall. Many missions have their bells set into arched walls rather than towers. The boy disappeared behind some shrubbery, and seconds later the deep, hollow call to worship echoed across the valley. The acolyte reappeared and descended the stairs, blowing into his cupped hands. In the morning chill, he had actually rung the huge, cold bells by pushing them with his bare hands. Such a primitive ritual in our modern world seemed charming to me.

While Lily fixed a hot breakfast after Mass, I tried to express gratitude by replacing a couple of burned-out light bulbs in ceiling fixtures that she could not reach. We ate heartily, but her generosity again exceeded my appetite. Then I had to be on my way.

It was the first of many partings, a dimension of pilgrimage that I had not considered before. Naturally I was grateful to her. But I was not prepared for my feelings of loss at leaving someone I had met only fourteen hours earlier. A bond had developed, too nascent to be called friendship, too personal to be called acquaintance. It dawned on me that the daily farewell would be an important humanizing element of the pilgrimage. It is a far cry from stopping at motels and restaurants. I would have to become personally involved with those who hosted me. Anything less would be gross insensitivity. Then every morning I would have to move on, leaving my new half-friends behind. Could I risk that psychic drain every day for six weeks? I had no choice. So with mingled thankfulness and sorrow, I said goodbye.

There is a scene in the Gospels in which Jesus is a guest at a dinner and an unidentified woman anoints him with expensive perfume. The Lord's host complains against her. Jesus retorts that wherever the Gospel is preached, the story of what she did will be told in her memory (Mk 14:9). That was how I felt about Lily. I was so moved by what she had given me, and not just the food and lodging, that I wanted to go out and tell people about her, how trusting and selfless she was. I was to feel that often in the next forty days.

My walk day began at 8:45. The weather was fine: sunny, and cool. Lily's directions proved excellent. The secondary roads she had chosen for me led north and west through La Jolla and out to the ocean at Scripps Medical Research Center.

I had not yet discovered my endurance pattern, so I did not have a rhythm for resting. I simply walked until I got tired, then sat down until I was rested. Breaks averaged about ten minutes every hour and a half.

The day went smoothly. Praying and walking sensitized me to the beauties of ice plant, wildflowers, hybrid purple daisies at freeway entrances, snowcaps inland, and cumulus formations overhead. There was plenty of time for the events of nature to happen to me, and nothing important to distract me.

At the Scripps Center I used the restroom and the water fountain. Sinking deep into a sofa in the spacious lobby, I became embarrassingly aware of not belonging. I was beginning to feel homeless again. Fantasizing an official-looking person requesting my departure, and fearing that it might happen, I got up and left.

Back on the road, the thirst that had led me into Scripps taught me that I was going to have to carry water. I had not foreseen that. I had planned to ask for drinks along the way, but it soon became clear that distances between them could get unbearable. Just as I was realizing this, I found a pint bottle by the side of the road. It was glass and had held orange juice. I picked it up and stuffed it into my pack as if it were treasure. My poverty was turning me into a scavenger.

I passed Torrey Pines Golf Course and descended to the ocean. It was a pleasure to walk the beach, mainly because it was soft. My knees were beginning to hurt from the pounding. As the afternoon wore on, I grew steadily more anxious about where I would spend the night. No mission this time. Would I have to go door-to-door? Or should I just give in and go to the rectory? Why not just go to rectories all the time? I was so repulsed by the prospect of begging shelter that my anxiety doubled. After wrestling with it for some time, I reasoned that God did not really want me to carry around all this fear and worry. He loved me and wanted me to have peace. So I would go to the rectory "just this once" and not feel guilty about it. After all, I was still new at this pilgrim stuff. I had to work into it gradually. I marvel now at how smoothly I talked myself out of my guilt over copping out. Jesuits have the reputation, whether justified or not, of being skilled rationalizers. I lived up to it that day.

Beyond the village of Del Mar, having covered twenty miles since leaving San Diego, I decided to seek St. James Rectory. The monsignor at the mission had told me that it was in Solana Beach, near the Del Mar line. My landmark was a racetrack. From a modest rise it came into view.

I needed to ask directions, but there were no houses on the main road. So I climbed a side road into a canyon. Here I found houses, but no people. For a reason I will never understand, I passed by the first three or four homes and turned instead to a modernistic wood-and-glass structure farther along. There was a car in the driveway. Maybe that attracted me.

My nervousness prevented me from even noticing the door nearest the street. When I came around to the side deck, I found a whole family at home: mother, father, and two pre-teen boys. They were all unusually friendly and cheerful. The parents spoke with an eastern European accent. When I told them I was a Catholic priest on pilgrimage looking for St. James Church, the father laughed and told me that I had picked the only Catholic family in the neighborhood and one of only about four families in Del Mar whose children attended St. James School. They gave me detailed directions and I headed off, puzzled at the coincidence and suspecting the hand of God.

Three minutes later I had company. The two boys swept down behind me on their bikes. They had gotten permission to walk me to the rectory so I would not get lost. The younger boy, Geza, was eleven and had a full head of blond curls. Bela was twelve, brown-haired, and definitely the quieter of the two. Both wore soccer shirts, shorts, and sneakers.

Questions ensued, like "What's a pilgrimage?" and "How far do you walk a day?" Geza broke a lull in the conversation by saying, "It's too bad you left so fast."

"Why do you say that?" I asked.

"'Cause my mom said it would be nice if you stayed for dinner."

I stopped walking. "She really said that?"

"Yes."

"Is it too late to go back?"

The boy paused ever so briefly. "No. Do you want to?"

Their eyes lit up, and so did mine. Without another word we turned the bikes around and went back up the hill.

The boys' parents were surprised to see me again, but ostensibly pleased. I was offered a glass of wine and plied with many questions about my pilgrimage. In turn, they told me about themselves.

The family was Hungarian. The parents, Endre and Julianna, had escaped from Hungary during the revolution of 1956, before they knew each other. They had been about twenty, I think. Endre had strapped leather-bound volumes of the writings of Guy de Maupassant to his forearms to use as skids and had crawled to freedom across the frozen Danube at night under rifle fire. Julianna had crossed Europe on foot, begging her way to the United States. After those experiences, taking in a pilgrim priest was only natural.

We ate heartily and I learned more about them. Endre and Julianna had both gone to Seattle, where they met and married. Endre became an architect. In fact, he had designed the house we were in. They were active Catholics who valued their faith and strove to pass it on to their sons.

As we ate, their intention to take me to the rectory, and my resolve to go, grew steadily weaker. It was finally decided by consensus that I would stay the night.

I asked about the boys' names. Bela and Geza had been ancient Hungarian kings. The boys were being brought up to cherish their heritage. They were also becoming accomplished soccer players. We talked about their school and sports, and after dinner we played pencil puzzles and even talked about God. Geza explained the Trinity to me: "That's where you have three all crammed together." More succinct than Aquinas, and probably as clear!

I called Casa Inigo and told my community how well the Lord had provided for me. Then Endre, the boys, and

28

I made a foray to the basement to bring up a mattress for the floor of the family room. This was a large, strange room with nooks and crannies in various directions. Up through the middle, from floor to ceiling, was a glass elevator-shaft affair. Through it grew the trunk of a large Torrey Pine called Herbie. The house was built around "him" because Torrey Pines are a protected species. I was told that Herbie would guard me during the night.

I showered and did some laundry. Before retiring I showed the family a Gospel text that had become very important to me, Matthew 10:40–42:

> He who receives you receives me, and he who receives me receives him who sent me. He who receives a prophet because he is a prophet shall receive a prophet's reward, and he who receives a righteous man because he is a righteous man shall receive a righteous man's reward. And whoever gives to one of these little ones even a cup of cold water because he is a disciple, truly, I say to you, he shall not lose his reward. (RSV)

During the period of doubts and temptations before beginning my journey, I had been reading Father Gerard Hughes' account of his own walking pilgrimage from London to Rome, *In Search of a Way*.[3] He had done it differently, taking a full complement of camping gear, food, and money for provisions. His goals were different. He explains that before he began his walk he was confused about the Church's role in the world and his role in the Church. He wanted time to think and pray and sort it all out. As I read, I noted that I was starting out from an interiorly different place. I was not in a time of turmoil or questioning. In fact, I felt happier and more secure in my relationship with God, the Church, and myself than I had for some years. My goals for the pilgrimage were to walk with Christ, to abandon myself to the Father's care, to let whatever happened be God's gift to me, and to imitate the Christ of the Gospels in whatever ways grace allowed. My ultimate desire was purification and transformation, so that Christ would live and walk in me. I wanted people who met me to meet Christ, too. It was these desires, combined with the passage just quoted from Matthew 10, that brought me to call the pilgrimage "Christwalk."

In my naiveté and enthusiasm I ignored the subtle arrogance my piety camouflaged. Ostensibly I was presenting myself as the disciple requesting a cup of cold water. In fact, I harbored a deep-seated longing to be appreciated as the righteous man and the prophet. I needed to be like Christ not so much because of my love for him as because of my lack of love for myself. I was not large enough to satisfy myself. I was like a child bolstering his ego by wearing a Superman suit. Though I had, indeed, articulated to myself a desire for purification and transformation, I had not yet begun to see what the nature of it would have to be.

Saturday, March 3.

I rose at 6:45. Endre, Geza, and I breakfasted on Danish pastry and *cafe au lait*. Bela joined us, still half asleep.

At 7:45, Geza and I were ready to move out. He had gotten permission to walk along with me if he took his bike for the return trip. I was glad about the early departure because there were twenty-five miles between me and Mission San Luis Rey.

On the way out I noticed a wall calendar with a brilliant color photograph of the Golden Gate Bridge. "With God's help, I'll be there before Easter," I mused. Deep down I wondered if I would make it. The memory of that picture came to me often during the following weeks as a symbol of hope.

Geza walked his bike beside me and discoursed at length about things that eleven-year-olds are interested in. While listening and commenting, I stuck my hand into my jeans pocket to check on my two dimes. I had been persuaded to take two when I left Berkeley, on the grounds that some pay-phones require twenty cents. I felt the first dime, then fished around for the second. No luck. Another try. Still no dime. Tried the left pocket. No. The back pockets. Then I repeated the whole procedure. It was gone. Half my fortune was lost. I must have left it on the sofa where I had put my things last night. Maybe it had fallen between the cushions. I stuck my hand into the front right pocket six or seven more times just to be sure. I cannot remember ever having valued a dime so much as at that moment. So this was what the poor woman felt like in Luke 15 when she swept her whole house in search of a coin.

I did not say anything to Geza because he would have ridden all the way home to retrieve it. If I had stopped to assess the situation, I would have seen that I could easily get another dime. Instead I magnified the loss to catastrophic proportions and became thoroughly distracted. Later that morning I found myself checking a phone booth to see how much it cost to make a call. Ten cents. I stuck my finger into the coin return chamber. It was empty. This was something I had often done in the past, out of curiosity or greed, but never out of genuine need. It reminded me of the bag ladies in the Boston Greyhound Terminal who go from phone to phone looking for change. I felt a prejudice within me begin to break down.

Geza and I were overtaken by Bela on his bike. He had decided to accompany us. Our conversation continued, and the boys unknowingly lured my attention away from the lost dime. They told me about kites and frogs, the nun at school called "Big Red" and their other teachers, and trains and surfboards. We were walking along the tracks up the coast, eager to wave to a train. None came.

31

Geza was more talkative than Bela. He asked why nuns live in "covenants." He also asked why I called my pilgrimage "Christwalk." But before I could answer, he proffered, " Is it because Jesus is in the grass and the trees and the sky? And in us?"

When we had walked about four miles, the path petered out just south of Cardiff Beach. It was a convenient place for the boys to turn back. Again the pain of separation closed in on me. In less than a day I had fallen in love with these boys, though they did not know it. We shook hands and they turned to go. At the last minute, Geza looked up and said, "You know, you're the first priest I've ever had for a friend." My eyes clouded with tears as we waved for the last time. Realizing that I would probably never see them again, I sat on the beach and cherished my sadness. Bela and Geza had shown me simplicity and trust. Their parents had shown me generous hospitality, learned at the cost of their homeland. Remembering them as I write this five years later, the feelings of gratitude, and of loss, still come back.

On the beach I reflected that my days would be measured by the separations. Rising in the morning was a continuation of the previous evening's relationship. My new day would begin when I left my hosts and took to the road. This day it happened when the boys turned back and I grieved. The nature of pilgrimage is to be constantly pulled into the present and toward the future. There is no holding on.

I walked as far as I could along the sand of Cardiff Beach. There were wetsuited surfers, some gulls, and a few swimmers and joggers. The sun, surf and breeze helped me recover my composure.

My heels and knees were hurting now. I judged it was time to put in a second layer of foam inner soles and the foam heel cushions I was carrying. They stayed in for the rest of the six weeks, and they were by no means a luxury.

Arriving in Encinitas about 10:45, I came upon St. John's Catholic Church. I had been looking for a charity to which to give the $5.00 from the priest in San Diego. The church was unlocked, but empty. No poorbox was evident. After my visit and a slug of water, I looked for a rectory. Across the street stood a building with a cross in front. It was a convent. A young sister in casual clothing answered the door.

"Good morning, Sister. Do you have some kind of fund for the poor, like a St. Vincent de Paul Society?"

She studied me suspiciously and pronounced a cautious "yes."

"Well, I'd be happy if you would put this into it." I handed her the five dollar bill.

"Oh . . . well, uh . . . thank you."

Starting to turn away, I remembered the second item on my agenda. "Oh, Sister, would you be able to give me a dime?"

Pause.

"Uh . . . yes, I think so." How could she refuse? She left and returned thirty seconds later. I thanked her and went my way.

Maybe I should have given her some explanation. But that would have been too complicated. She made out all right on the deal, and I was back to my original twenty cents. My steps felt lighter now that I was not burdened with those five dollars. Having money made me feel powerful and compromising. If I were to be really poor and dependent on God and his people, I could not carry money. In my pilgrimage proposal I had stipulated that I would beg money only if necessary. If I received unneeded cash I would give it to the poor as soon as possible.

For the next few hours I walked the Pacific Coast Highway, with the Atchison, Topeka, and Santa Fe tracks on my right. This was surf country, and the villages were

33

lined with surfboards and bronzed young men in straight, yellow, shoulder-length hair.

Beyond Ponto the road became tedious, and my legs were hurting. I prayed the Jesus Prayer slowly in step, but the Lord seemed far away. "Lord . . . Jesus . . . Christ . . . Son . . . of the living . . . God . . . have mercy . . . on me . . . a sinner." Over and over. "Why do I feel this way? Ah, yes. The newness is wearing off." That was it. I began to think about how long six weeks could be. "Yes, six more weeks of walking. Forty-two more days. Alone. Foolish. Not romantic at all. Just hard."

I stopped at another beach to eat a cheese sandwich I had left over from yesterday's lunch. Nearby a young couple were embracing on the sand. Desire and envy coursed through me, and I felt keenly my need for intimacy and caring. My solitude had devolved into loneliness. I tried, with modest success, to distract myself with recollections of how often Jesus held me close to himself, and in how many ways: in Lily and the Hungarian family, in my Jesuit community, and in the quiet of prayer. None of these thoughts negated the loneliness. It was an inevitable feature of the lifestyle I had chosen. Better to know it by its true name than to repress it under a pious veneer.

Leaving the beach, I plodded on to Oceanside, where I turned inland on Mission Road. Since it was Saturday there would probably be an evening Mass at the mission, which I wanted to attend, so I poured on the steam for the last five miles. Two miles in, I crested a rise overlooking San Luis Rey Valley. Below me a green, fertile flatland rolled away to the distant hills. It was lush and inviting under the deep blue sky. My heart leapt as the sun danced off the white of the mission three miles away. First sight of my goal. Home! I was standing on a *mons gaudii*, a "hilltop of joy," so called by the medieval pilgrims of Europe when they got their first glimpse of the shrine to which they were traveling. This was the first of many times I would feel this exhilaration. It arrested me, and I wanted to stand there and thank God for the mission. Reality swept in and called me down the grade. On the flat, the last two miles seemed twice as long, since I had already seen my destination. I was weary and hot, and rather irritated at the distance, and I tried to pray, but could not. All I could do was murmur "Christwalk" every few paces. For one brief moment I felt united with Christ as I approached the mission, and I believed Christ was approaching it in me. It made the effort feel worthwhile.

It was 5:28 when I reached the front door of the church, and indeed there was a 5:30 Mass. I had wanted to concelebrate, but when I found that the pastor was already vested and on his way to the front of the church to begin the procession, I abandoned my desire. I did not want to be a nuisance at the last minute. The ushers out front kept assuring me it would be no trouble. They were so insistent that I agreed to let one of them take me around the outside of the church to the sacristy. On our way we ran into the pastor, a Franciscan, who was just as welcoming as the ushers. They stowed my gear in the baptistry, and I went down the side aisle to the sacristy. Having vested hastily, I entered the sanctuary through a side door just as the pastor was arriving the long way. All this took about sixty seconds.

When I sat down for the readings, it was the first time I had relaxed since Oceanside, and I was not sure I would be able to stand up again for the Gospel. My concern was justified. It took all my energy and concentration to stay standing. I did not hear the reading at all. Through the whole liturgy I was distracted by weariness, and what praying I did was simple thanksgiving for being warmly received.

When we stepped outside after Mass, the priest's first words to me were, "Would you like a place to stay tonight?" It was a relief not having to repeat my San Diego ordeal.

It was the pastor's custom to greet the parishioners in front of the church after the liturgy. While he was doing that, an agitated young man came out of the shadows and caught my attention. "Is there anyone here who can give me some counseling?" he asked me.

"I'm afraid I'm just a visitor here, but I'd be glad to try to help you if I can."

"Well, I just came to church here, and I've been away from the Church for seven years."

"Would you like to come back?" I inquired.

"I don't know. If I come back I'll have to go to confession, and I'm afraid the priest will kill me."

"I see. Well, I can assure you that no matter what you've done, I won't kill you. My job as a priest is not to judge you. It's to try to show you the kindness and healing of Jesus. I'm sure the pastor here is the same way. Would you like to meet him?"

He hesitated, then said, "Yes, I think so."

I introduced them to each other and went back to the sacristy. I do not know what happened after that, except that the pastor was with the young man a long time.

I thought about how many people are outside the Church and are afraid to come back, afraid of the priest. Is it the fault of the clergy? If we succeeded in being more like Jesus, would there be more people in the Church today? But then, every Christian is called to be like Jesus, to give the kind of love he gave. So it cannot be just the clergy's fault.

After dinner I had to get permission from the superior of the Franciscan community to spend the night at the mission. He was a tall, rugged Brother with graying hair. Before becoming a Franciscan, he had been a forest ranger. He heard my story and asked if I had identification. Having seen it, he matter-of-factly offered me bed and breakfast.

"Where are you heading tomorrow?" he inquired.

"I'm not sure. What is there between here and San Juan Capistrano?"

"Not much. Just Camp Pendleton. They'll let you walk through. San Clemente's about the first place you can stop. There's a parish there. But it's about twenty-eight miles."

This conversation planted seeds of ominous concern in my mind. Tomorrow would be a tough day. At the time, I had no idea how tough.

Sunday, March 4.

My day began with a hearty breakfast, after which I stashed away a banana and some bread. No one offered me a lunch for the road, and I was still too new at this to know I should ask.

Because it was the First Sunday of Lent, I stayed to concelebrate at the 9:00 parish Mass. It was a good experience, but it put me on the road at 10:00 A.M., at least two hours later than prudence would have dictated, considering the distance between me and my next lodging.

I started in good spirits. The sun was out, my feet felt all right, and my knees were not too bad.

Praying the Jesus Prayer that morning led me into deep recollection. It stayed with me up the long hill to Oceanside. The trek back to the Pacific I considered time and energy lost, since I was only doubling back on ground I had covered the day before. This galled me a little, but I tried to accept it as part of the Lord's plan. We do a lot of doubling back in life.

The marine sentry at the south gate of Camp Pendleton checked my I.D. and approved my passage to San Clemente, remarking that it would be a long walk. I did not need another reminder.

There is no reasonably direct route from San Luis Rey to San Juan Capistrano except through the marine base. The whole coastline for twenty miles, and a good fifteen miles inland, is military reserve. Interstate 5 cuts straight through it, but pedestrians are prohibited from freeways. The walking route is roughly, very roughly, parallel to it, with much dipping and winding. My direction markers were the little blue and white signs for the Pacific Coast Bicycle Route.

Walking through Camp Pendleton was like walking through wilderness, and it was the first appreciable stretch of it I had encountered. There were none of the usual marks of habitation, such as billboards or road signs—just an occasional oil-drum trash barrel marked "Compliments of Weapons Training Unit 4." The land was bare, comprised of flat terraces and low rolling hills, with higher hills ahead to the right. Occasionally I was reminded of my whereabouts by a rifle shell underfoot.

This wilderness suggested to me the desert in the prophecy of Hosea. The Lord says to unfaithful Israel:

> So I will allure her;
> I will lead her into the desert
> and speak to her heart. . . .
> I will espouse you to me forever:
> I will espouse you in right and in justice,
> in love and in mercy;
> I will espouse you in fidelity,
> and you shall know the Lord.
> (Hos 2:16, 21–22, NAB)

I mused that the Lord might be leading me out to his trysting place, where he could take me for his lover. I desired that. As the hours crawled by, however, I did not feel romantically infused with the Lord. Instead I grew increasingly lonely.

Except for a slight haze in the distant hills, the air was clear and fresh. It was getting hot. My face, neck, and hands were beginning to burn. That was another problem I had not prepared for. A small one, however, compared with the length and barrenness of the road.

The day dragged on and my feet grew progressively more tender. Out of necessity I began to develop a little savvy about walking. For instance, I found myself looking for favorable surfaces. Much of Camp Pendleton had fine sandy dirt along the edges of the roads, and I tried to stay on this rather than on the pavement. A peculiar bootprint kept appearing in this dirt, like a waffle-iron with circular indentation. The tread stayed with me so long that I joked to myself that it must be my guardian angel.

At last I came to a sentry gate. The clock read 4:00 P.M. I asked the sentry to verify my position on my map. His finger touched Las Pulgas, which I thought I had passed long ago. The Las Pulgas gate is an entrance to Interstate 5 only halfway through the base. I was at least five miles behind where I had estimated. Crestfallen, I tramped down to where the bike route became the old unused bed of U.S. 101. It was overgrown with weeds along the edges, but excellent for biking or walking: flat and straight.

After about half an hour, I had to leave the roadbed briefly to negotiate an overpass from I-5. Coming around it, I got a sad surprise. I could see far in the distance the tiny, hazy outline of a nuclear power plant. It was the size of a small pea, and I estimated its distance at ten miles. Between it and me was nothing but wilderness and old Route 101. In desolation I let out a long, whining, "Oh, no!"

Annoyed and anxious, I tried to quicken my pace, but my legs were too tired. I was beginning to lean on my staff and use it to push the pavement behind me. I was also beginning to limp. This was the second consecutive twenty-five-mile day, and I was not yet in shape. With the sun getting lower, there was no question that I would be walking in darkness. "Hard to get lodging after sundown," I reminded myself.

An hour later I felt more sharply the urgency of sunset. It would get cold and damp and very dark, unless there were a moon. I could not remember what phase the moon was in. How would I be able to stay on the bike route in the dark? I would be wandering in the brush and losing time. A row of posts separated the north and south bike lanes from each other. I could use the end of my staff to feel them and stay in the center. No, a little ahead the pipes disappeared. Maybe the faded white center line would still reflect a little light from the headlights on I-5, or from the moon if there were one.

Up ahead two men had parked a shiny black Trans AM and were photographing it against the Pacific and the lowering sun. The clear orange disk hung an inch above the horizon.

"Can you tell me how far it is to San Onofre?"

"Where?"

"San Onofre."

Silence. Puzzled glances.

"Isn't there a town called San Onofre up there by the power plant?" I asked anxiously.

"Oh, yeah. San Onofre. It's about three or four miles straight ahead. This road goes right to it. You can't miss it."

"Is it military or civilian?"

"Oh, it's civilian. Yeah. Stores. People."

"Thanks a lot."

Three or four miles. I could make that by seven or seven-thirty without too much trouble.

Sunset was about 6:00. I reached a public bathhouse with sinks, toilets, and showers. It was locked, but there were two sinks outside connected by a counter. The water ran. I guessed it was built to serve the bike route.

The setting sun was red and beautiful, but I could not enjoy it much. I was too concerned about the fast-chilling air. I put on my sweater, windbreaker, and navy watchcap, then sat up on the counter between the sinks to get out of the wind and off my feet. I was shivering. It would be wise to move along soon. Walking would keep me warm.

Unlike New England, southern California has a very short twilight. I found myself in rapidly fading light almost immediately after the sun had dropped behind the horizon.

As I was leaving I noticed the number 14 on the side of the bathhouse. Through the dusk I could make out a similar structure in the distance ahead. Between them were wide, numbered parking spaces painted diagonally across the southbound lanes of old Route 101. It came to me gradually that this stretch of the highway had been converted into a trailer campground. The next bathhouse was number 13. Judging by the distance between bathhouses I computed the park to be two miles long. Its entrance became my next immediate goal, reasoning that I would find civilization nearby.

The park was not entirely unused. A few scattered campers were battened down for the night. At 6:30 I came upon a family with a campfire behind their trailer. They let me sit and warm myself.

"How far is it to San Onofre?" I asked.

"Oh, five or six miles."

That news jolted me. I had not been prepared for such a change in estimates. Apparently the two men with the Trans AM had just been getting rid of me.

At 7:15 I reached the gate of the trailer park, having passed a dozen campers with lights on inside. I had sorely wanted to knock and seek shelter, but I did not dare inflict myself on people with such tight quarters.

It was totally dark, and quite chilly. The lights of the nuclear power plant were coming close, but reaching them was cold comfort. When I got there, not a soul was to be seen. Just lights and chain-link fences. Leaning into my stick for momentum, I hobbled past the enormous structure. It seemed to mock me. It stood as a monument to broken promises. I was still without a place to spend the night.

My mantra became, "Though I walk through the valley of the shadow of death, I will fear no evil. Thy rod and staff give me strength." I repeated it many times. The power plant fence seemed to go on for more than a mile.

At last a small home-like building appeared, with lights burning. No, just a government outpost. As I limped past it, a jeep rolled up behind me, the first moving vehicle I had seen in hours, except for the distant headlights of I-5 still on my right. I felt beaten, but hopeful, as I approached the driver. He was a Border Patrol officer. After explaining my situation, I asked about the town of San Onofre.

"No town here. Just the power plant."

"Then how far is it to the nearest homes where I could get lodging?"

"About four miles. The first one is Nixon's."

I was too exhausted to be impressed. I felt as if I could not walk four yards, much less four miles. My legs and feet were screaming for mercy. Could the officer please drive me? No, it was forbidden to take passengers in an official vehicle. He suggested that maybe a surfer or forest ranger would pick me up. I pleaded. He held his ground.

I dragged myself forward. When would this night be over? Everything seemed to be against me. I hobbled another hundred yards. Suddenly I had company. A dark figure was rising out of the brush ten feet to my right. A man. Coming toward me. I could not make out any weapon, and he seemed to be alone, but for a moment I thought my ordeal was about to end.

"You a cop?" asked the stranger in a Mexican accent.

"No. Who are you?"

"David."

He was a wetback. The pickup truck that he had driven from Tijuana had broken down nearby, and he was hiding from the Border Patrol. Despite the scare, he turned

42

out to be another gift. Fresh and energetic, David walked much faster than I. Though I had to strain to keep up with him, he was bettering my chances of getting lodging. At the same time I knew that I probably would not get a ride or a place to stay if I had a companion. A mixed blessing.

After a quarter hour with David, I had to rest. He was going too fast for me and I was about to fall over. I sat down on the ground with my back against a chain-link fence. David went on alone. I devoured a Three Musketeers bar that I was still carrying from San Diego and thought of the warm bed at Lily's apartment. For a few seconds I even thought that death might be a relief. My feet throbbed, and above the ankles they burned where the lips of my boots were chafing.

As much as I wanted to stay right there, I knew I could not. Pulling myself to my feet with my staff and the fence, I clumped forward. A few times I thought I sensed a car coming from behind, but when I turned to wave it down, there was nothing but darkness.

In an attempt to pray, I recited the words to the song, "Be Not Afraid." It seemed to say what I really needed to hear.

> You shall cross the barren desert, but you shall not die of thirst;
> You shall wander far in safety, though you do not know the way. . . .
>
> If you stand before the power of hell and death is at your side,
> Know that I am with you through it all.
>
> Be not afraid. I go before you always.
> Come, follow me, and I will give you rest.[4]

Several real vehicles did drive by, and I waved frantically to get them to stop. In anger and despair I cried aloud, "I'll never pass by a hitchhiker at night again!" My tone ironically reminded me of Scarlett O'Hara's, "I'll never be hungry again!" Promises uttered at such a pitch are rarely kept. I have not kept that one.

The next words out of my mouth were, "My God, my God, why have you forsaken me?" All of a sudden I understood that phrase as I never had before. How could Jesus, with his intimate knowledge of the Father, say those words and really mean them? That had been a problem for me. But in my present state the problem dissolved. My head knew and believed that God was present and loving me all along. But my feet, my stomach, and my heart did not feel it at all. It was they that were crying out.

I climbed a ramp to a bridge over I-5 and flagged down another Border Patrol jeep. I begged for a ride to the nearest Catholic church. No ride. The officer told me that just across the bridge was a gate to, of all places, Camp Pendleton. I did not want to hear that. I was feeling very down on the military. The Border Patrolman suggested that I call the Catholic rectory on a pay phone that was near the gate. Good thought. I started to cross the bridge. Just then a little sports car came off the freeway and pulled to the side of the road. I darted toward it. A window rolled down, and a young couple peered out.

"I'm in trouble. Can you help me?"

"If we can. What is it?"

"I'm a Catholic priest. I've just walked twenty-five miles and I can't go any farther. I have no money and no place to stay tonight, and I need to get to the Catholic rectory in San Clemente. Can you drive me there?"

"Sure. Hop in."

Those three words held so much power. Suddenly I felt safe.

The driver was a young lawyer from L.A. He and his girlfriend were driving home after a day in San Diego. This being the halfway point, they had pulled off the freeway to change drivers. The Lord had come through for me after all.

We stopped at a gas station for directions to the church. It was about three more miles. They dropped me off at Our Lady of Fatima Rectory at 9:00 P.M. and drove away. At that point I thought my trial was over, but it wasn't quite. One last scene had to be played out.

I rang the rectory bell and waited. No answer. Rang again. Still no answer. Third time. Footsteps. A thin, middle-aged, Irish priest opened the door about eight inches and listened skeptically to my story. He did not know whether or not to believe me. I volunteered my I.D., but he declined it.

He seemed not to want to let me in. After an awkward pause in which he seemed to be deciding to turn me out, I heard my own voice quavering in absolute powerlessness, "Please don't send me away." It came from such depths that he responded immediately, "I'm not going to send you away." It was over.

The priest was the pastor of Our Lady of Fatima. He actually had no bed for me in the rectory because a deacon had moved into his last empty room. He would arrange, however, for me to stay at a motel just down the hill. After letting me call Berkeley, the pastor gave me directions to the motel. He also gave me $5.00 for food, which I had not asked for. I thanked him and wearily descended to the main street. Half the money got me a hamburger, fries, and a strawberry shake to go. Around the corner the motel manager was expecting me. He showed me to a suite: two rooms and a bath, with my choice of three beds, twins in the front room and a king-size in the back. How my fortune had changed in one hour!

I ran some hot water in the tub and set a chair facing it. When I got my boots off, my feet were covered all over with red blotches, and tiny blisters had formed above my ankles where the edges of the boots had rubbed. With my feet in the tub, I ate part of the hamburger and some of the fries, but exhaustion had stolen my appetite. Besides, I was feeling shivery in my shoulders and feverish in my head. Not wanting to get sick, I soaked my whole body in hot water until the chill went away. I almost fell asleep in the tub. After that I went straight to the king-size bed. I think it was about 11:00. With barely a word of thanks to the Lord for getting me here safely, I was asleep.

Monday, March 5.

It was probably about 7:30 when I awoke. I remember thinking it was much later because I had slept so deeply. Though I felt rested, I was not recovered. My muscles were sluggish and my feet were tender. There was no fever or chill, for which I was thankful, but I was far from having my usual vigor.

Returning to the rectory to thank the pastor, I was admitted by a slender, attractive woman about my own age. Her name was Joyce and she spoke with a Florida accent. While I waited for the priest, Joyce gave me a cup of coffee. A moment later the pastor entered and exclaimed, "So you *are* for real! The fakers don't come back." The whole atmosphere had changed. I was treated like a homecoming hero. Joyce, who I think took mothering lessons from Lily, set out a lumberjack's breakfast and then proceeded to amass a lunch for me that I could not fit into my backpack. Before I left, the resident deacon and a couple of parishioners pressed me to accept some cash for the road. I explained my policy about giving it to the poor. They still insisted, and gave me a total of $15.00. I felt rich, considering I still had $2.50 from the pastor, plus my dimes. On my way down the hill, the street sign caught my eye for the first time. Our Lady of Fatima Rectory was on a street named La Esperanza: "Hope."

The weather was sunny and clear, and it was getting hot. Though I had not left my hosts until 11:00 A.M., I was not worried. I had only seven miles to walk today, five north on the Pacific Coast Highway to Capistrano Beach and two inland to San Juan Capistrano. It was a relief to have such a short day ahead of me.

Cradling my lunch like a newborn baby, I started north. Progress was quite slow because of my battered condition, the extra burden of the lunch bag, and the heat. Sheer cliffs flanked the highway on my right, catching the sun's heat and reflecting it. The temperature did not help me feel any better. My inflamed feet kept telling me to sit down and take the boots off, which I did often. It took me two and a half hours to walk the five miles to Capistrano Beach. But that was all right. I was in no hurry. I had done more than my share of pushing the day before.

To pass the time, as well as to forestall future calamity, I did an autopsy on the previous day's experience. Multiple errors, combined with a few uncontrollable circumstances, had led to my plight. I had failed to ascertain beforehand a true destination and had underestimated the distance. That ignorance had caused me to start out too late. It had been the second consecutive twenty-five-mile day on legs that were not yet conditioned. I had been weakened by eating sparingly and hoarding food, rather than consuming as much as I needed and relying on God's providence for replenishment. Finally, I had not allowed for the effect that prolonged wilderness would have on my psyche. Though entirely plausible, my analysis had a major hitch. I was placing on my own shoulders the burden of responsibility. The presupposition seemed to be that if I did everything right, the pilgrimage would proceed without difficulties. But life is not like that. My head knew it, but my gut resisted it. I have in me a strong drive to achieve security and happiness by controlling my environment. Just letting the world happen to me is very hard. I want everything to be a task that I can accomplish. The main challenge of pilgriming would be to relax and let myself be led.

I set foot in the town of San Juan Capistrano at about 3:15.

A young woman asked playfully, seeing my pack and staff, "Who are you—Tom Sawyer?"

I was so sweaty and fatigued that her humor was lost on me. "No. I'm walking the missions."

Her tone changed. She seemed pleased and a little impressed. As she went her way she tossed back, "Praise the Lord."

Her parting words made me regret not being in the mood for conversation. I did reflect, however, on her initial observation. Wasn't Tom Sawyer a marginal character? Didn't he refuse to get swept into the maelstrom of competitive society? He was a pilgrim in his own right. And generations of Americans have admired him and wished they had his freedom and simplicity.

At the mission rectory I was received graciously by the diocesan priests and immediately offered a room, a shower, and time for a nap. The pastor, a charming man who radiated joy, asked if I wanted to stay an extra day to rest. That prospect gave me pause. If I lingered the following day, would I reduce my chances of getting to Sonoma? There it was again, the temptation to achieve. I decided to take my cue from the Lord. If my feet were still inflamed the next morning, I would stay.

I concelebrated the 5:15 parish Mass and joined the priests for dinner.

That evening I stepped backward in time. It happened that on this day the parish was being visited by one of the seven "pilgrim statues" of Our Lady of Fatima. She seemed to have followed me from San Clemente. At 9:00 P.M., the four-foot polychromed wood replica of the Blessed Mother was being ceremonially carried out of the church in procession, and I was invited to vest and walk with the clergy. The church was full of worshipers. To the rhythm of the chant, "Adios, Madre del Cielo" ("Goodbye, Mother of Heaven"), the Madonna swayed on its litter the length of the church and out to the side street. I had seen such processions in movies from Spain, Mexico, and South

America, but I was unprepared to find one in modern California, much less be part of it. The simple piety of the candle-bearing parishioners penetrated me. It so differed from the dry intellectualism I had encountered in seminaries, schools of theology, and even in some of the religion courses I had taught in high school.

Then something turned sour. The black-suited layman who was in charge of the statue, and who had overseen the proceedings with the deftness and professional air of a funeral director, broke the mood of prayer. A young woman was stretching out her hand to reverence the statue, and the man barked, "Don't touch! Don't touch!" She pulled back her hand as if she had been burned. Jesus had said, "The sabbath is made for people, not people for the sabbath." The same can be said of statues.

When the man had packed the Madonna safely away in his station wagon, he engaged me in conversation. He boasted that he traveled all over the world "with Our Lady," and proceeded to refer to the statue as "she" and "her." I wondered at how an object made of wood could displace, say, the Eucharist or concern for the poor. It spoiled the evening for me.

Tuesday, March 6.

I woke up hungry. A good sign. I was thinking about my stomach instead of my feet, which meant they were better. When I looked, the inflammation was gone. I decided to leave the mission after the eight o'clock Mass.

I had been thinking about my father and stepmother the day before. The postcards I had brought to mail home were still in the bottom of my pack, and I had been out almost a week. Maybe I should phone. So I placed a collect call to Florida. With Dad and Jean being an older and more conservative couple, I did not know how they would take to my solitary, penniless pilgrimage on foot. All I had told them earlier was that I was making a tour of the California missions and would be on the road for all of Lent. I did not want them fretting. During this phone call, and later ones, I revealed to them little by little the parameters of the experiment. Today I told them that I was alone and walking. That was enough for a start. As for my condition, I was always "fine."

I preached about my journey at Mass, after which an old man in a wheelchair gave me a dollar and the younger man pushing him gave me five. As usual, I tried to refuse. They insisted. The pastor gave me ten dollars and asked me to offer two Masses for a special intention, specifying that one of them should be at Carmel Mission, where Fr. Serra is buried. On my way out, the associate pastor handed me another three dollars from a parishioner.

Now I had $19.00, plus some change left over from San Clemente. After farewells, I slipped to the poorbox and began stuffing the money in. A passing temptation slowed me down: keep a few dollars in case of emergency. No. That's not trusting the Lord. So it all went in. I left the mission with my two dimes.

The sun was high and I was going to have another hot day. Leaving the mission was like stepping out into the desert again in more ways than one. Besides the heat, I would have to cover almost seventy miles to get to Mission San Gabriel, my first three-day stretch. Today's goal was Corona del Mar, a suburb of Newport Beach about twenty-two miles ahead. There was a Catholic parish there, which gave me a feeling of security.

I prayed the fifteen decades of the rosary as I had done on the two preceding days. This became a daily habit throughout Christwalk, always with the same two prayer intentions: thanking God through Mary for food and lodging the night before, and asking for the same again tonight.

My right knee was beginning to give me trouble, so much so that I had to stop periodically to rub it to reduce the pain. I was walking with a limp and using my stick as a crutch. The curbs in Laguna Beach seemed unbearably high. A few must have been ten or eleven inches. Every time I tried to step up or down at a corner, I would get a sharp shot in the knee.

Responding to the pain, my prayers were mostly mantras to Jesus and Mary for relief, plus the song, "To you, Yahweh, I lift up my soul, O my God." Despite the throbbing, I was encouraged to see that prayer was becoming simpler and more spontaneous. With less conscious effort, I was growing in familiarity with God.

My timing into Corona del Mar was ideal. Late afternoon. I stopped at an Italian delicatessen to ask where the Catholic church was. They were not sure. Someone gave me vague directions, indicating that the parish center was about five miles away. It was a cinch I was not going to walk there now. The trial that I had been anxiously resisting was upon me. I would have to beg from door to door. It was an essential of pilgrimage, yet every ounce of me rebelled.

Back in December I had begun to have fantasies about doors slamming in my face and my having to sleep out on the ground. I asked a friend, a deeply committed young Christian wife and mother, what she would do if a stranger in jeans and backpack came to her door asking for lodging as a Christian pilgrim. She said her first inclination would be to want to take him in. Then she would be afraid. Who was he? How did she know he was not a robber or rapist or murderer. So she would call her husband and they would try to decide together. But she, a prayerful and active Christian, could not give me a definite answer. What would I meet at the doors of the less sympathetic?

I decided to use brain rather than brawn in Corona del Mar. Entering a residential neighborhood I studied the houses, looking for a sign of Christianity. I was hoping for something like a garden Madonna, a dashboard Jesus, or a charismatic bumper sticker. I found the third. Two blocks down I came upon an orange van with "Praise the Lord" and the fish symbol on the rear bumper. It was parked beside a dark-red house. I rang the bell. A young man came to the door, with a woman and a small child behind him.

"Excuse me. Is that your van?" I asked.

"Yes, it is." Puzzled look.

"Well, I saw the Christian bumper sticker and thought you might be able to help me. My name is Richard Roos, and I'm a pilgrim . . ."

As soon as I finished my story, the young man invited me in. I almost could not believe it. It seemed too easy.

I answered a few questions and told them my full identity. Their names were Patti and Robert, and their seventeen-month-old son was Ryan. They were born-again Christians, having joined Calvary Church because of its feeling of community and its vibrance of spirit. Patti had been a Catholic before. They invited me to go to their Bible Study group that evening, which I agreed to do. Then, seeing how hot and sticky I was, they offered me a shower.

When I came out from the shower, something had changed. Patti was gone and Robert had set a single place at the kitchen table. He gave me soup and cheese and crackers. Then he broke the news to me. They had gotten second thoughts about my staying overnight. The shower, I suspect, had been to get me out of the way so they could talk. I took the decision calmly, remembering my ace-in-the-hole, the church. It had gotten dark, so there was no question of begging at other houses.

Poor Robert was apologetic about turning me away. I assured him I understood his reasons. His first duty, I reminded him, was to his wife and child. He gave me fruit for my pack and asked if there was anything he could do for me. Yes, he would be happy to drive me to the rectory. It was about 7:00 when he dropped me off.

Corona del Mar is a well-to-do town, and the church is in one of its better residential districts. The parish complex appeared to be modern and affluent.

I rang the rectory doorbell and waited. No answer. Tried again. Still no answer. A circling of the building and a third ring convinced me that no one was home. It was Tuesday and possibly the priest's day off.

There was activity in the school. C.C.D. classes were beginning, but no sign of a priest. I returned to the rectory and tried the bell once more. Again no answer. So I sat on the stoop and took out my Bible. It never crossed my mind that I might be there for hours. I was confident that the Lord was going to provide for me. It was as simple as that.

About twenty minutes later, an attractive couple arrived, perhaps my age or a little younger. As they approached the bell, I told them of my failure to raise anyone. The woman rang anyway. When no one came, they decided to wait along with me.

We exchanged pleasantries, then went into telling each other about ourselves. They were Linda and Bill, engaged to be married, and seeking a priest to discuss the pre-nuptial procedures and paperwork. They had tried several times to contact the parish priest, but he was never available. They had no appointment this evening, but thought they would take another chance.

After we had traded stories and Linda had tried the bell a few more times, they got tired of waiting. We had been there together about twenty minutes. Seeing their frustration and disappointment, I offered to take their names and a phone number and have the pastor call them. They gave me Bill's number, adding, "If no one comes in a little while, you call the number and we'll come and get you." I liked that idea, but it was immediately pre-empted by a better one. "On second thought," Bill said, "why don't you just come with us now?"

Linda was twenty-six and worked at U.C.L.A. as an administrative secretary. Bill, an architect, was thirty-five. They both like to travel, and Bill's place was full of souvenirs from around the world. He had been on Truk in the Peace Corps and was particularly fond of Polynesian art.

They both wanted to hear more about my walk. Bill could not get over my doing it without money. He shook his head. "Most of us spend all our time trying to get money, and you go around giving it away!"

From the very start there was an electricity between us. That meant a lot to me, because they had not had good experiences with the clergy before.

They asked all kinds of questions about the Church's regulations regarding marriage and the wedding ceremony. We talked for almost three hours, during which I walked them through the entire pre-marital interview and advised them regarding dispensations they would need. Finally Linda asked, "Where did you come from?"

"Berkeley," I reminded her.

"No . . . I mean, you're exactly what we needed. And you just dropped into our lives out of nowhere! How did you get here?"

"Don't you know?"

"You mean . . . ?" She raised her eyes slowly toward the ceiling.

"I believe it," I admitted.

A respectful silence descended on the three of us.

Wednesday, March 7.

Linda was at the apartment again before I left. It was her custom to take Bill to work each morning before going off to U.C.L.A. We talked some more about their wedding, which they thought might be in late summer or early fall. Bill took a memento snapshot of me with my backpack and stick. Then it was time to go. I was getting that heavy heart again. There was something so natural about our relationship. The couple had opened their lives and their deepest concerns to me very quickly. Given more time, a strong friendship could have grown. We all sensed it. So leaving was especially hard that day. When the hugging and waving were over, however, and when I was on the road toward Huntington Beach, I had an unexplainable intuition that I would see them again. It may have been just an indulgent wish, but it came true. Five weeks later, when I arrived home in Berkeley, a letter from Corona del Mar was waiting for me. Bill and Linda had a favor to ask. Toward the end of August, on the last day of my year in California, I witnessed their marriage.

Shortly out of Corona del Mar my right knee acted up again. The pain made my spirits drop, and their descent was accelerated by the premonition that my progress would be considerably hampered.

I had decided to aim for Buena Park, eight miles northwest along the coast, then fifteen miles inland directly north. That would take me away from the Pacific, which had been a daily companion. Knowing that I would not see her for a week, I became nostalgic.

The fifteen miles I had to walk on Beach Boulevard were dead straight, lined with shopping centers, and no shade. By early afternoon I was hot and bored, and my knee was so bad that it shot pain each time I brought the leg forward for the next step. I discovered that a good way to reduce the shock was to keep the knee rigid and use my staff as a cane running down the outside of the leg. I looked like someone trying to walk with a full leg cast, but that did not bother me. What I feared was breaking my stick from the extreme pressure I was putting on it when it hit the pavement. I had grown attached to that companion, too, even more than to the Pacific.

At 4:00 P.M. I had just entered Stanton, only halfway to Buena Park. I prayed the rosary for my usual intention, then tried to cope with the pain by offering it up to God as a sacrifice "for peace in the world and wisdom in the governance of the Church." That phrase became my mantra.

The rhythm of my gait was steady, but the tempo was too fast. I was pushing myself to get to Buena Park. If I did not get there today, my connection between San Juan Capistrano and San Gabriel would have to be four days instead of three. That would put me a whole day behind schedule. "Behind schedule?" What schedule? I was doing what I had done before: prodding myself compulsively forward. The Lord was saying to me, "Slow down. Do it my way." But doing it his way would mean that I would have to admit that he loved me as I was, with my limitations. I did not want to be limited, however, or at least not as limited as I perceived myself to be. That was a symptom of not really loving myself as I was. Since I was good enough for God, why was I not good enough for myself? God was telling me that I did not have to make it to Buena Park today. Success meant following his calls each hour of each day, not attaining a goal that I had pre-set for myself.

Pride, then, is an underhanded enemy. It creeps into everything, even the service of God. It wears a thousand masks, even the mask of humility. I overwork and drive myself in his name, when I am really serving only the expectations I have laid on myself in order to be acceptable to myself.

Recognizing that to press forward would be to give in to a compulsion, I decided to cut the day short. My inner peace returned. On another level anxiety over my homelessness began to crystallize, as it did almost every afternoon for the entire six weeks. Would I find a home tonight? Here in the city what kind of danger would I be risking if I had to stay outside? My fear of falling sick from the cold came in second to my fear of being mugged.

Feeling vulnerable and insecure, I choked up at the thought of knocking on doors. I reached for the easy way out. A woman on a ladder nearby was pruning shrubs.

"Pardon me, ma'am. Do you know if there's a Catholic church anywhere near here?"

"Up at Katella. Two blocks ahead, at the second light."

Well, it was the third light, and in my condition that made a difference. In the East we refer to a block as a four-sided cluster of buildings with a street on each side. Along Beach Boulevard, however, a "block" was the distance between traffic lights at major intersections, disregarding all other side streets. The distance was usually two-thirds to three-quarters of a mile. So Katella was a full two miles from the shrub lady.

I also found out that when people want to get rid of you, they underestimate the distance to your destination so you will feel encouraged and be on your way. "Only a few blocks up that way" can mean anything from two to five miles. It would have been funnier if my legs had not been in such distress.

Anyway, I prayed to Mary for strength and repeated my mantra, "For peace in the world and wisdom in the governance of the Church." Eventually I reached Katella. No church. Why was I even looking for a church? Because I was still afraid to beg from door to door. I was angry at myself for feeling that way, but it was the truth.

I approached a nearby taco stand and asked about the Catholic church.

"Oh, that's back on Chapman, left at the Jack-in-the-Box."

Chapman was where I had been before, and I sure was not going to hobble *back* two miles. I did not know whom to be angry at—the shrubbery lady, the taco boy, or God—so I directed my fury into energy for walking. I decided that the Lord must mean for me to move forward, even in my painful state and even though he had just seemed to be asking me to give up Buena Park. After two more "blocks," or about a mile and a half, my right leg was screaming for me to stop. I finally listened.

There was a side street with small shabby houses. I started to look for one with a sign of Christianity or welcome. Until that moment I had not realized how choosy I was. I could have knocked on a dozen doors, and at worst the occupants could have said, "Go away," perhaps slamming the door in my face. I would have been no worse off than I was now, not even having the courage to approach the doors. "The foxes have lairs. . . ." When you have nothing, there is no place to go but up.

My pride got the best of me. I preferred to plod up and down the street wrestling with myself and waiting for lodging to be handed to me on a platter the way it had been at Lily's and the Hungarians'. It did not happen. The honeymoon was over.

Looking back, I am ashamed of the fear that kept me from asking for what I really needed. I was far from the humility I desired.

I am also ashamed of the prejudices that I became aware of that afternoon. As I scouted the neighborhood, I felt uncomfortable about staying with non-whites or non-Christians or the poor. My white, upper middle class, New England Catholic background was blocking me. I kidded myself that I did not want to impose on the slender means of a low-income family, but what really held me back was my aversion to inconvenience. I was not up to a night in a small, noisy house, possibly crowded with children. My stereotypes were strong. I rationalized that my battered condition necessitated the comfort of a rectory.

Resisting the temptation, I approached a well-dressed young man sitting outside drinking a can of Budweiser. He was watching two little girls play in the yard.

"How do you do. My name is Richard Roos. I'm a Christian and I'm making a pilgrimage of . . ."

When I got as far as mentioning that I had fallen short of Buena Park, the young man cut me off and said, "Oh, you're almost there. It's only two blocks up. Once you cross Lincoln, you're in Buena Park." I took the hint.

I returned to the boulevard without knocking on a single door. It was not fear of rejection that prevented me, however. I was not afraid of what people might say or do to me. It was what they would think of me. My stumbling block was that I might be considered a liar or a fool. I could survive being turned away; it was being misunderstood that I could not endure. That would be a deeper, more personal rejection. It was not the first time, nor the last, that my need for respect kept me from preaching the Gospel.

There is a line that separates saints from ordinary people, a line that the saints have chosen to cross. The territory beyond that line is seen by the prudent to be folly, by the rational to be insanity, and by the envious to be outrageous freedom. It was that line which, as much as I wanted to, I could not cross. The reason I could not was precisely that I wanted to, that I could see the line. The saints who cross it cannot see it at all. They do not know that they are different. They know only that they do what they have to do, impelled by love.

Lincoln Avenue was indeed two blocks up, or another mile and a half. By the time I arrived, it was completely dark.

On the corner of Beach and Lincoln was a gas station with five teenage boys inside. I stuck my head in and addressed the boy at the desk: "Do you know where there's a Catholic church?"

"I know where several are." He was impressing the others.

"Where's the nearest?" I was not amused.

"Up at Orangethorpe—about two miles."

Testing him I asked, "What's it called?"

"Pius the Fifth." He probably meant "Tenth." A forgivable error.

At last I had a destination. I had swallowed my guilt about not going door-to-door and was deliberately seeking another rectory. Being actually within the city limits of Buena Park lifted my spirits somewhat, though I was still waging a losing battle with my leg. My prayers for relief did not seem to be working. Maybe if I changed the prayer . . . I recalled that there was a network of friends praying for me all over the United States, as well as in Canada, France, Haiti, and I could not remember where else. The communion of saints.

"Lord, if my own prayers are not powerful enough to relieve this pain, then please inspire someone to intercede for me whose prayers will be more effective."

Then with an uncanny belief that I was not just wasting my breath, I stumped along saying audibly, "Someone out there, pray for me." After several minutes I got the idea that I should try to walk without my crutch. To my amazement the pain had almost entirely subsided. I needed only to favor the knee a little. My pace picked up and my mantra changed to one of thanks.

Not long after that I found St. Pius V Rectory. The boy had been right. Why had I doubted?

The young girl at the reception desk summoned a priest in his seventies, a semi-retired ex-missionary who had spent most of his priestly life in Africa. I had landed in a community of Irish Augustinians, and my effusive host treated me like a long-lost nephew. He fed me, served my Mass, and told me stories of the twelve African countries he had labored in. To top it off, he lodged me in a spacious, two-room suite with private bath. It belonged to the pastor, who was visiting Ireland. It felt good to soak in a hot tub again. One thought, however, rankled me. I had again run for the safety of a rectory.

Thursday, March 8.

Morning started out misty and cool, but soon the fog burned off and the day turned sultry. The air was heavy with smog.

Although leg pains had bothered me throughout the night, my knee was notably stronger. For the first time in a couple of days I was able to walk without the aid of my staff. That prompted me to contemplate the psychological effect of overdependence on artificial helps. It could exaggerate my sense of weakness. Using my stick only when necessary could teach me my real strength, and also my real limits.

My thoughts turned to the condition of my legs. They were in fine shape for walking, but they were not much good for anything else. The walking muscles had grown strong, but for other movements they were stiff and sore. Stepping on or off curbings was torturous. The L.A. curbs must have been the steepest in the world. Some of them seemed two feet high.

Putting my boots on or taking them off was a problem, also. I would sit on the ground and try to bend my legs up so I could reach the laces. They would not respond. It was as if they were paralyzed. I would have to grab the undersides of the knees with my hands and lift them to get the legs to bend. It did not hurt. The legs just would not do it on their own. It was almost as if they had minds of their own and were saying to the rest of me, "All right, we'll walk for you, but that's all. Don't give us any other orders. We won't obey them."

That imaginary ultimatum led me to think of St. Paul's comparison of the Church with the body of Christ (I Cor 12:12–27). Each organ and limb must help the others in cooperative unity, or the whole organism suffers. If the legs do not go forward, neither do the arms or the head. That is true of all organizations and institutions, but it is especially true of the Church. As the body of Christ we are united not only on the natural plane, but also on the mystical. We are incorporated into the universal *persona* of the risen Christ. We are all one. As a community of faith, the holiness of the whole is enhanced or diminished by the greater or lesser personal holiness of each of the members.

On the practical level it seems that, if the holiness of the Church is directly proportional to the personal commitment of the members, then perhaps it needs rites of initiation that involve greater personal choice. The Church suffers from the apathy of many peripheral members who were inducted without their own consent. If infant baptism is to be continued, then confirmation ought to be stressed more forcefully as a rite of passage into adult membership. Also, we need to develop a theology of baptism for infants that includes the sponsoring adults as recipients of the grace of the sacrament. Thus the sacrament would be seen to enable the mature members to nurture the infant member in the necessary faith of the community.

Finally, consider the California missions, which had been nascent churches. As microcosms of the universal evangelizing mission of the Church, why had these institutes failed? Why had their lives been so short? Why were there no surviving Christian communities of native Americans that could be traced back to them? The missions had been founded on a two-pronged socio-religious theory: no salvation outside the Church, and European culture is suitable for everyone in the world. Church and state were wedded in the missions for political and economic ends. The natives of California were Christianized and Europeanized in such a way that they became religious colonials, easily dominated by the Spanish crown. No attempt was made at inculturating the person of Christ into the religious heritage and experience of the natives. How could Christianity have been expected to perdure? Only in our own generation is inculturation being addressed as the major missiological issue in Africa. If we believe that the message of the Gospel is truly universal, then we must accept it as trans-cultural.

Not long after noon I was thoroughly distracted by the sun's merciless heat. Any shade was a blessing. The only protection I had for my head was my navy watchcap. Beyond any doubt, I was going to need a hat.

I prayed: "Lord, give me a straw hat. I need one and I believe you want me to have one. Tell me how to get it."

A minute later the idea came. If I found a Goodwill or Salvation Army thrift shop, I would go in and look for an old, unsalable straw hat and ask for it. Less than half an hour later, I found a Goodwill Shop on Whittier Boulevard. I did not even have to cross the street. Within thirty seconds I had spied an old Mexican sombrero with its high pointed crown ripping away from its wide brim. There was no price tag. The hat lay on a trash heap. The cashier sent me to the manager, who heard my story and was happy to part with the hat. She even offered me some tape to repair it, but I declined. I wanted to do a more permanent job with needle and thread.

The sombrero fit fine, but looked ridiculous. The wide, half-detached brim flopped up and down in rhythm with my steps. I was more conscious of my appearance than of my prayer. People stared out of cars and pointed. In addition, I had no chin cord. With its broad brim, the sombrero kept blowing off in the slightest breeze. I definitely would have to work some creative alterations when I got to Mission San Gabriel. For the moment, at least, I was relieved to know I would not die of sunstroke.

When I turned on to Rosemead Boulevard, traffic was heavy. My stupid hat embarrassed me even more, flopping to the beat of its own drummer. It was a relief to turn left on the more deserted San Gabriel Boulevard. My self-consciousness was a good lesson, though. It made me aware of my vanity. Human respect more than once tempted me to risk the heat of the sun rather than look a little laughable. How often in the past had I opted for appearance rather than reality?

The boulevard turned north toward the mission and became a wide city street lined with apartments. The sun was getting low and I was beginning to feel my usual anxiety about lodging. It was clear to me that if I wanted to avoid walking in the dark, I would have to fall short of the mission and settle for arriving the next morning. I felt ambivalent. The mission was only about five miles ahead, according to the map Lily had given me in San Diego.

Still not convinced that it was the right thing to do, I started scouting for an inviting-looking place. Again I felt the inner embarrassment about not simply going from door to door. When would I be free enough to do what I knew I was called to do?

I was in a Spanish-speaking neighborhood. Not knowing the language, I went farther north. Two women walked by and I asked if there were a church ahead. Yes, St. Anthony's was "just on the other side of the freeway." That would make it about two miles.

Before getting there I went up a side street. It was still light. Two women were conversing through the screen door of a red house. I approached them and stood expectantly about three feet away. They ignored me. The woman inside wore a small gold crucifix at her throat, and I hoped she would see the metal one hanging on the front of my shirt. They were speaking English. After two or three minutes, they finished. The outside lady went away and the inside lady disappeared into the house. Neither acknowledged my presence. I had become invisible.

I had experienced this once before. A few months earlier I had tried panhandling near Union Square in San Francisco to see what it felt like to be that far down. I had let my beard grow for three days and had put on old clothes. I pocketed my eyeglasses because the metal rims looked too affluent. I would walk up to people and look them in the eye, and they would pass right through me as if I were not there. Losing my identity and the visibility of my own body was the most humiliating poverty I could imagine.

Undaunted by the woman's unceremonious exit, I knocked on the screen door. The woman's voice told another person to answer the door. A tall young Mexican came to the screen. I told my story.

"We have no room here, but is there anything else we can do for you?"

I was hungry. "Could I have a piece of fruit?"

"Yes."

He left and I heard him rummaging in the refrigerator. Then he came back. "No fruit, but here's a tomato. Anything else?"

I thanked him, then asked how far it was to the mission.

"Not far. A mile or two ahead, then left on Mission Road a few blocks."

I thanked him again and headed up the boulevard. My feet had begun to hurt. The heels were tender and I had developed a large blister on the top of my left big toe.

If I had looked ridiculous before, it was worse now. I was limping, using my stick as a cane; my sombrero was flopping up and down; and I was chomping on a tomato. I hoped the mission would appear soon.

After another mile or two I was thirsty, but my water bottle was empty. I should have asked for a refill at the tomato house. Too late now. I tried a nearby gas station. The attendant was another young Mexican. I leaned on my stick and said, perspiring, "Pardon me. Do you have any water?" I mimed drinking from a glass.

"Yes. Water. My water," he said, pointing to the cola machine and studying my crucifix.

Not sure what he meant, I went on, "May I have a drink?"

He went to the cooler and withdrew a twelve-ounce bottle full of cold water. Realizing that it was his own water and was probably all he had, I put my hand up to refuse and backed away. He called me forward and held out the bottle. I sipped a little and tried to hand it back, but he shook his head vigorously and repeated the command, "Drink!" I guzzled more than half the contents of the bottle. It tasted delicious. The selfless generosity of this stranger, with whom I could barely communicate, touched me deeply. The Gospel promises recompense to "whoever gives even a cup of cold water." It does not say, "gives the only water he has."

Darkness closed in soon after that. I turned left on Mission Road and began the "few blocks" to Mission San Gabriel.

After what seemed like an hour I came to a wide intersection with a railroad track running through it. In the dark on the far side of the square loomed the outline of a massive curved facade. Mission San Gabriel Arcangel! Suddenly I had that warm, safe feeling again.

Getting inside the mission was a chore. The front was completely dark, with no evidence of a door. I walked cautiously to the right, around the far corner, and to a lighted back door. It was the rear of the rectory. A woman let me in and showed me to a large kitchen. The Claretian community that ran the mission was just finishing dinner. A balding priest in an open-necked clerical shirt was scooping ice cream in the kitchen. I told him who I was and that I had left San Juan Capistrano three days earlier. He caught me off guard by interrupting and saying drily, "I see. And now you want directions to Mission San Fernando?" For an instant I was at a loss; then I saw that he was joking. He readily granted my request for lodging.

The Claretians gave me a hearty supper, which I ate in the company of two Jims and a Larry, Claretian novices. Then I showered and washed my clothes. The stretch from Capistrano had been long, and I was extremely tired. While lying in bed writing my journal, I fell asleep.

Friday, March 9.

That morning I rose late. There was no need to rush out. Mission San Fernando was only about thirty-three miles away, and that meant two short days of about sixteen or seventeen miles each.

My first thoughts were about the push from Capistrano. In the last three days I had walked twenty-two, twenty-three, and twenty-four miles. In eight days I had covered one hundred and fifty-seven miles. My legs felt bad. *I* felt bad. I realized that I was still too attached to getting to San Francisco. Christwalk was not supposed to be a forced march, but a prayerful, restful pilgrimage. Being "on the way" was the main thing. "If I make it only half way," I had said, "but learn humility and prayer, then it will be all worthwhile." The distance walked was intended to be quite secondary. But I had forgotten that. I was still succumbing to the temptation to be an achiever. The story of my life has been one of "rush and wait" or "push on and collapse." Such behavior could defeat the purpose of pilgrimage. To avoid being physically overcome, emotionally drained, or spiritually desolate, I would have to establish a healthy rhythm. That would be the key to endurance. The heartbeat, the breath, the waves and tides, the seasons, and even human generations—all perdure through rhythm. It gives security and peace, the comfort of regularity. I must not let my compulsive, task-oriented nature ruin the experience. I could conceivably press myself forward to Sonoma and achieve nothing but a tour de force. Yet my stated goal was spiritual, and spirituality thrives on mellowness, inner peace, and rhythm. The walking must not be done "to get there," but simply "to be here" with Jesus. I was glad for the two short sprints to San Fernando. They would give me a chance to try practicing what I preached.

At breakfast a Claretian brother engaged me in conversation when he heard me mention the Jesus Prayer.

"What does it mean," he asked, "when the Gospel says not to use a lot of words when we pray?"

"It means," I explained, "that we shouldn't try to impress God with the fine rhetoric of our prayers. Be simple. Be yourself. Don't try to impress others, because that's vanity. And when you're alone, don't try to win God's favor by wordy prayers. God loves us just as we are. We don't have to earn his love." I should have listened to myself.

The brother rejoined, "But God would love us more if we were what we're supposed to be."

"God can't love us more. He already loves us perfectly," I objected gently.

The brother mused further, "I sometimes wonder why God loves me. I don't do anything to deserve it."

"God's love," I countered, "is like the love of a mother for her newborn baby. The infant hasn't done anything to deserve the mother's love. All it's done is be born. Everything else is noise and mess. But the mother loves the baby with all her heart. She'd die for it."

The brother did not carry the subject any further.

After breakfast I went back to my room to fix my sombrero. A small plaque on the wall caught my eye:

Lord, fill my mouth with worthwhile stuff,
And nudge me when I've said enough.

I hoped I had not said too much at breakfast.

Alterations on my hat were simple and effective. First I cut about three-fifths of the brim off with a razor blade. Then I sewed the crown and brim together. Next, I gave the tall pointed crown a vertical karate chop down the middle from front to back. Suddenly my sombrero had become a Panama. Last, I strung one of my extra boot laces through the holes where the original chin cord had been. I then had a Panama that would not blow off. The long boot lace would also serve to hang the hat from a loop on top of my backpack when I was not wearing it. Poverty breeds ingenuity. My hat was no longer an eyesore, nor a distraction, nor a burden. I was quite pleased with myself.

After celebrating Mass in the old church, I toured the historical restorations of the mission. One item in the museum section caught my eye. It was a painting of a beautiful young woman in a full flowing gown staring at her reflection in the mirror of a vanity table. The mirror was rather elliptical and disproportionately large. The entire composition formed a death skull, with the mirror shaping the cranium, the woman's head and its reflection marking the eyes, a lampshade outlining the nose, rows of perfume bottles suggesting the teeth, and the antependium forming the jaw. The title of the work was the famous line from Ecclesiastes 1:2, "All is vanity." The painting seemed to say, "Vanity is death, and death ends all vanity." But life is the freedom that comes from putting vanity to death. I was so enamored of my insight, and of my resolve to murder vanity, that I was blind to the vanity itself. Even altering the hat had been to protect my pride. I was far from the simplicity of heart that I had set out in search of.

I packed up and was ready to leave at 11:15. The cook had prepared an outlandishly generous lunch: four sandwiches and three pieces of fruit. I accepted it all, having learned the hard way not to refuse food.

Smog kept the day rather overcast, and walking was decidedly uneventful. Because of my short goal, there was less pressure on me to keep up a pace. A slow rhythm enabled my reflections and meditations to unfold freely.

First I thought of how pilgrimage was a healthy reversal of my usual lifestyle. I had grown accustomed to being the controller, the one with power, the independent man, the person who gives freely to those who come to him in need. On the other hand, I had always had a hard time receiving from others, especially when I had nothing to give in return. On the road I was coming to terms with my own need for others, need that was as basic as food, shelter, and acceptance. If I chose to, however, I could escape the full force of that dependence by retreating into my priesthood and falling back on the security and comfort of rectories. I had let fear drive me to that several times already, and I hated it. When would it stop?

These considerations, plus a collection of less developed thoughts, accompanied me to where Colorado Street intersected San Fernando Road in Glendale, halfway between the missions. The day was pretty far gone, so I stopped to seek lodging. Daylight would last another hour.

I had been struggling so much with the fear of begging door-to-door and with my guilt over using rectories that I sensed a crisis coming. Something had to erupt into either a breakthrough or a total collapse.

While this churned around inside me, I walked slowly the length of a residential side street looking again for some Christian symbol. There was none. My anxiety level was high. I was determined not to go to a rectory, yet I was petrified at the possibility of rejection and humiliation. I longed to be self-possessed, humble, and free of my need for acceptance and approval. St. Ignatius had said that the best thing to do when trying to be rid of a fault or overcome a limitation was to act against it, to take bold and positive steps in the opposite direction. That was what I wanted the courage to do.

Across the street was a large two-story house with a sign hanging out front: "CERAMICS . . . Open. Workshop in Rear."

"Ah! Artists!" I told myself. "They'll be outgoing and imaginative."

Going around to the shed which served as the shop, I found it unlocked, but empty and dark. Hearing the back door of the house open, I turned to see a middle-aged couple coming down the steps. They looked neither altruistic nor welcoming. On the contrary, they looked annoyed and suspicious. I introduced myself and remarked that I had seen their "Open" sign out front. Then I launched into my prepared speech about the pilgrimage and my need of lodging. They listened without expression. As soon as the last syllable dropped from my lips, the man swayed his head back and forth looking at the ground, sliced the air with his hand and said, "I've got too many girls here to take a chance with strangers in my house. You'd better get goin'." I thanked him politely and left. By the time I had gotten around to the front of the house, the woman had come through to the porch and was removing the sign. I felt like a schoolboy flunking an exam.

A few blocks farther on I met a young man in his late teens walking a very young puppy. I played with the puppy, then asked if he knew where there was a Catholic church. I thought it would be handy to know. He could not help me. Then I told him my story and asked if he could take me in. He did not say "no," but he would have to ask the other three guys he lived with. One of them came along, and between them they decided that I should go to the church. The second young man told me it was Incarnation Church and was on Glenoaks and Brand. I had passed near it a couple of miles back. Since I had no appetite for backtracking, I encouraged myself to keep trying private homes, though all the time moving in the general direction of the church.

A lady with a Christian fish symbol on her car had a kind attitude, but she could not help me because she was going out that evening. It was Friday, and I guessed that a lot of people would be going out. She, too, directed me to Incarnation Parish.

A block away I tried a house on a corner, having skipped half a dozen. The lady who listened to me sent me four houses down to her friend, "who's a Catholic." Her friend just told me to go to the church. By now it was getting dark. After all these invitations to Incarnation, I gave in and went there.

It was 6:30 and dark when I rang the rectory bell. The woman who answered put me in a waiting room because the priests were at dinner. Ten minutes later a friendly young priest came out and listened to my story. He disappeared for a few minutes, returned and asked for some identification, then disappeared with it. He was gone a long time. I got worried and began to wonder what I would do if they turned me out. I prayed for a "yes" and felt my powerlessness. "The Son of Man has nowhere to lay his head." Eventually the young priest, whose name was Jim, returned and said I could stay. He told me that the parish gets many strange visitors and the pastor had been wary of me. They had called Loyola High School across the city to verify my identity. Whoever answered the phone had the presence of mind to check the California Jesuit Catalog, in which I was listed as a member of the Casa Inigo community. That had saved me.

Jim showed me to a guest room. I called Berkeley and talked with Ed. Both of us were disappointed that I was at another rectory. Ed encouraged me to be more decisive about going from door to door.

Either success or defeat had to be imminent, I felt. I could not go on disappointing myself much longer.

Saturday, March 10.

I woke up as angry at myself as I had been the night before. This evening I would stay at Mission San Fernando, a mere sixteen miles away. Tomorrow, however, I would not darken the door of another parish house. Come hell or high panic, I would beg from door to door—like a *real* pilgrim.

By 9:30 I was making my way northwest along the grassy median strip of Glenoaks Boulevard. The bright sun portended another hot day. My feet and legs were in good shape, except for the blister on my left big toe, which was still full of fluid.

I was $15.00 richer now, having given Jim the $5.00 from San Gabriel for the St. Vincent Fund and having received $20.00 from a parishioner after the 8:30 Mass.

That seemed to be the pattern. Whatever I gave to the poor, more came to replace it.

My thoughts turned to some discouraging predictions Jim had made about the Cuesta Grade north of San Luis Obispo and the wilderness of the hill country beyond. He had said I could expect to spend a few nights out on the ground. My throat tightened as I envisioned desolate mountains, loneliness, hunger, cold, sickness, and possibly the absence of God. While the net of fear was entangling me, there came, at a deeper level, an intimate touch from the Lord. I was reminded that I was doing all this for him, and I could feel a power pulling me forward. It was like opposite currents flowing at different depths in the same stream. Along with this I felt an inner communion with Jesus in his conflict at Gethsemani, seeing the probability of suffering, and experiencing the power of love within that makes it both endurable and worthwhile.

The day's walking was uneventful. The only incident was my being hailed by a wino from a doorstep. It was about 3:00 P.M. and he was well oiled. Spying my crucifix, he started pumping me with questions about why I wore it and what I was trying to prove and where I was walking to. When he learned that I was heading for the mission and was on pilgrimage, he became argumentative.

"You think you're going to find God at those missions," he announced, "but you're not. You're just wasting your time walking all over California looking for God. You should have stayed home! That's where you'll find God. And yourself. You're probably looking for yourself, too! Well, forget it. Go home! Look at me. I stay home and I know who I am. You know who I am? I'm an alcoholic, that's who. But at least I know who I am."

When I was finally able to get a word in, I tried to calm him down. I assured him that I was not trying to find God or myself at the missions, but that my pilgrimage was a walk *with* the Lord who was already with me and was in me all the time. That pacified him.

I reached Mission San Fernando Rey de Espana at 4:05 P.M. according to the clock in the gift shop. The mission is an historical attraction, but does not function as a parish. Rather it is occupied by diocesan priests who run a seminary high school on the property. Since it was Saturday, all the resident priests were away serving in parishes. One of the ladies staffing the gift shop rang several priests' rooms on an intercom phone, to no avail. No one was home. I could not stay at the mission.

As this news sank in, I began to see the hand and humor of the Lord. He was going to test my resolve today, not tomorrow.

I told my story to the gift-shop lady, but she could not help me. Her apartment was small and she was in the process of moving. She was sorry.

With more courage and calmness than I would have predicted, I walked out to the main street and turned toward a row of houses that I had passed on my way in. I was determined to do it today. Every house, till someone took me in.

I went to the first house. No answer. At the second they listened kindly but had company that evening. They gave me a glass of water because I was sweltering. Third house, no answer. Fourth, polite refusal. Each bell I rang got easier. Fifth, "Sorry, we don't have room here. But you should skip the next few houses and go to the corner. I'll bet they take you in."

Accepting that advice, I went to the corner house. A boy answered. I asked for his father, who appeared momentarily. He was a big man in early middle age. I told my story and reported that no one was home at the mission, concluding, "Would you have a sofa or some corner where I might spend the night?"

"Sure. Why not? We don't have a spare room, but I'm sure we can find a corner for you somewhere."

I think I was more surprised at his response that he was at my request. He acted so matter-of-fact about the whole thing.

My host's name was Don. He lived with his wife, Ginny, and their two teenage sons, Mark and Steve. Don was building a swimming pool in the backyard, so I spent some time watching him and asking questions. I tried to play some handball with Mark, but my legs would not permit it.

I was surprised to find that our dinner conversation remained light. Though they had opened their home to me, the family members were relatively private. They were interested in the externals of pilgrimage, but seemed uncomfortable with overtly religious connections.

After the meal we watched television and ate popcorn. The family made no attempt at further conversation, though their demeanor toward me was friendly and accepting. I felt uncomfortable. They were treating me like a normal member of the household. It was almost disappointing.

On the other hand, I had time to reflect on the breakthrough that had finally come. Another corner of the wilderness had been tamed. I had not been laughed at or slammed out. The unknown had been exposed, and begging door-to-door had shown itself not to be the sleeping dragon that I had anticipated. People had been kind, even those who had refused me. They had returned my gentle politeness with an equal measure of the same. In addition to finding that I could rely on the Lord's strength within me, I was learning that I could also count on his grace in the hearts of those to whom he would lead me. With that the back of my fear was broken.

Ginny prepared Mark's bed for me, and Mark slept in Steve's room. In the privacy of the bedroom I wrote in my journal. I was feeling not only thankful for the place to sleep, but also thoroughly satisfied with the way I had gotten it. I was becoming the pilgrim I had set out to be. Yes, I had relied totally on the Lord. In my euphoria I again missed the vanity that tainted the victory. I was crediting myself with my reliance on God.

Sunday, March 11.

Don was cooking sausage and eggs when I emerged from Mark's room at 7:30. The rest of the family was still asleep. While we ate I asked Don what had persuaded him to let me stay at his house. "Spur of the moment decision," he answered without hesitation. "I'm a good judge of character and I rarely make a mistake. You seemed O.K.—and I was right."

I returned to Mission San Fernando and concelebrated at the 9:00 Mass. The homily bothered me. It was about Abraham being asked to sacrifice Isaac. The preacher's whole message was that God puts us on earth to test us. I do not buy that. It makes God sound like some kind of mad scientist in the sky who creates people as a game to see which ones can make it through the obstacle course of life. It is frighteningly similar to the attitude expressed by King Lear, "As flies to wanton boys are we to the gods. They kill us for their sport." If God is love, then all he has to give is love, not testing. Everything he makes or allows to happen to us must be out of perfect love. He can give us no less than what is best for us, even if we do not understand it at the time. Everything works toward our growth in love and holiness.

After Mass the lector, an older gentleman, asked if he could give me some money. Instead of accepting it, I gave him the twenty dollars I had carried from Glendale, suggesting that he make a donation to his favorite charity. He was taken aback. Beggars are supposed to take money, not give it away. Then he named an orphanage in the south-eastern United States and said he would be happy to oblige.

To leave the mission I had to pass through the gift shop. The woman who had tried to help me the day before was on duty again. She told me that some people had tried to find me last evening. The family of one of the girls who worked in the shop had wanted me to stay with them. Two homes on the same night!

The day's walking was pleasant and uneventful. The weather was sunny and warm, but not hot. My legs felt good, the only problem being that blister on my left big toe. It had broken during the morning. I was a bit concerned about infection, but decided to leave it in the hands of the Lord.

My route took me through Chatsworth at the west end of the San Fernando Valley, up over the Santa Susana Pass, then down into Simi Valley. For the next three days, until I reached Ventura, I would be heading directly west.

Ambling toward the Santa Susana Hills, I noticed that my concept of progress had changed. I no longer measured my advances as I had when I drove a car. The number of hours between major cities or state lines was irrelevant here. As a pedestrian it was a major event to discover what lay on the other side of the next hill, and I had the luxury of wondering about it for hours. The snail's pace contributed greatly to the contemplative experience. Prayer was simple, often completely without words. Communion with Jesus was as effortless as breathing, and frequently as unconscious. We were just together.

At about 4:30 I rested on a bus-stop bench in a residential neighborhood of the town of Simi Valley. Since my map showed me to be roughly a third of the way to Ventura, I decided to look for a place to stay. My daily cloud of apprehension had descended, but yesterday's victory had given me new courage and self-possession. I turned into the first side street I came to and started begging door-to-door. By this time I had explained myself so often that

I had a memorized speech. It seemed to work, so I stuck with it. It went like this:

"How do you do. My name is Richard Roos. I'm a Christian, and I'm making a walking pilgrimage of the old California missions. I started in San Diego and I hope to make it to Sonoma by Easter. I pray as I walk. When I come to a mission, I stay with the priests there. But when I'm between missions, as I am now, and when the sun is getting low, I seek lodging from whoever will take me in. I don't carry any food or money. Instead I try to depend entirely on the goodness of God and the people I meet along the way. Do you think you might have a sofa or a cot or some corner where I might spend the night?"

Then I would wait.

Only later did I recognize my little speech's potential for provoking interior crisis. Naturally, many sloughed it off. But others, even among those who would refuse, gave it serious thought. Should they believe me? Maybe they remembered assaults they had read about in the papers. If they were Christian, perhaps they recalled Gospel passages about helping the needy. Parents would think of their children. All this took less than fifteen seconds. A stranger, by asking to be trusted, had brought them to a critical moment of decision that put them face to face with their humanity, their philosophy of life, their belief in God, or whatever else governed their value system.

Here in Simi Valley I recited my piece and was turned down at the first house. No one was home at the second. Some children were playing on the lawn of the third house. I talked with them for a moment, until their mother came into the yard from up the street. She listened intently to my story and seemed to want to take me in, but she could not make the decision. "Why don't you try a few more houses, and if you don't get anything, come back. My husband will be here in a few minutes. You'll know he's home when you see a yellow VW out front."

There was no answer at the fourth house, but while I was ringing the bell, the yellow VW arrived. I walked back and met the gentleman on the sidewalk.

"Pardon me, sir. Is this your house?"

"Yes, it is."

"My name is Richard Roos, and I just spoke with your wife. She told me to come back when you returned. I'm a Christian making a walking pilgrimage. . . . "

The man listened with interest, then shook his head and said in a friendly tone, "Not this trip." I wanted to ask him when he thought I would be by again. Later I saw my mistake. I had jumped the gun. I should have let him get inside to hear about me from his wife. They would have talked it over and she might have helped my case. If it happened again, I would move more slowly.

The lady in the fifth house was friendly, but was "already booked up with weekend guests."

At the sixth house a young woman's voice from inside said, "Come in." Not sure I should enter, I knocked again. The invitation was repeated, so I pushed the door open and stepped inside.

"Oh, I thought you were one of us!" said the young woman. She was seated at a dining room table with a few people her own age and one older couple. On the table lay the remnants of a child's birthday party. Two small girls were playing nearby. All were dressed in their Sunday best.

I excused myself for interrupting, then told my story. One of the young men, the husband of the woman who had invited me in, took charge. He introduced himself as Rick. He was in his twenties, thin, with short light-brown hair and moustache, and wire-rimmed glasses. He and his wife Kim were celebrating their daughter Carie's fourth birthday. The others were relatives, including Rick's parents. His mother reminded Rick a couple of times that there was a Catholic church in town, but Rick did not seem to hear her.

After inviting me to sit down at the table and offering me some food, Rick asked if I were a born-again Christian. I replied, "Sort of." We talked a bit about my wanderings, and I commented on how well people had been treating me. At that point Rick and I got into a discussion about whether or not people are basically good or evil. Based on the fall of Adam and the accounts of sin in the Bible, coupled with the history of sin in the world, Rick took the position that humans are basically evil and that the purpose of redemption is to save us from our real selves. Based on the account of creation and on the doctrines of the incarnation and grace, I tried to defend the intrinsic goodness of human nature. I did not get very far. Rick's interpretation of Scripture was literal and his beliefs were fundamentalist. Almost two weeks later, at the mission in San Luis Obispo, I recalled this conversation and carried it further in my mind. If to be human is to be intrinsically evil, then the Son of God could not have become truly human, because one who is the perfection of goodness cannot "become" something evil. Besides, if sin is an essential part of our humanity, then forgiveness and salvation make us less human. That cannot be. Salvation makes us more fully alive, more fully human, and more fully ourselves.

My debate with Rick was cut off by a scramble to get ready for church. In my case it meant taking a shower.

The service was in a tiny match-box of a church. It was a branch of the Tennessee Church of God, an old high-pentecostal denomination.

At one point in the service Rick asked me to stand and give a witness talk about my pilgrimage. When I introduced myself as a Catholic priest and a Jesuit, there was a ripple of discomfort through the congregation. I went on to explain that I had begun my journey because I had felt Jesus calling me to prayer and surrender to his Spirit. I was talking their language. The tension eased and the people were with me the rest of the way.

80

Back home, Rick and Kim had no guest room. Rick improvised a mattress of blankets on the living room carpet, topped with a sleeping bag. It was quite comfortable. His last gesture was to close the front curtains and apologize for the glare that might come through. It was his custom to leave the porch light burning.

"For security?" I asked.

"No," he replied. "If you were out in the dark and in trouble, which house would you go to for help?"

"The one with the light on."

"That's right. I leave it on every night. You never know when someone will come."

Monday, March 12.

Rick worked in a chemical plant at the end of his street, so after a hot breakfast we walked together to the corner. Before we parted he took seven dollars out of his wallet and insisted that I take them. Five were to be used "for the work of the Lord, like buying Gospel tracts and handing them out, or something." The other two were for myself. I explained what would probably happen to the money, but he urged me to take it anyway.

I was beginning to feel less awkward about accepting money. It was not being given to me because I had asked for it or had manipulated people into offering it. It was not even being given because people thought I needed it. If anything, it would have been clear to people that money was the last thing I needed or wanted. I saw then that people were offering cash as their way of participating in the pilgrimage. They could not go with me, so knowing that I was carrying their money to the poor was their way of vicariously becoming pilgrims, or at least of affirming the value of what I was doing. They could "own a piece of the rock." I gradually learned to accept donations without resisting. By the end of Lent people had given me almost

$220.00, most of which I passed on to charities along the way.

Near the west end of Simi Valley I passed a mobile-home park that had two signs out front. One said in large letters, "FRIENDLY VILLAGE." The second, in smaller print, read, "Private Property—Keep Out." I wondered if the proprietors were aware of their inconsistency.

For several hours I wound through low hills on a narrow, lonely road that would take me to Moorpark and Somis. My heels were hurting, but not severely. I tried to stay on the soft gravel by the side of the road. A strong headwind slowed my progress.

Trekking through a wide valley that afternoon, I was visited by an image of Jesus as a benevolent giant walking around me in a vast circle, stepping from hilltop to hilltop. It was a phantasm that I had conjured up in the past, symbolizing the Lord's presence and power protecting me. At other times I experienced Jesus within me, filling me, like a rose whose blooming has been accelerated on thirty seconds of movie film. Beginning inside my feet and moving up through my legs and torso, he would reach out through my arms and into my head, until every inch of me was permeated. These moments did not last long, but their effect, which did, was important. They strengthened me for the down times that lay ahead.

The Southern Pacific tracks were on my right. A long freight train barreled past, giving me a feeling of exhilaration and freedom. I felt like the ten-year-old who runs down to the tracks every day after school to wave at the 3:27. Acting the child I waved to the caboose man, and he waved back. Such a little thing, but comforting at the moment—a human exchange on a lonely day.

I did feel lonely, and I was feeling bad about the length of the pilgrimage. It was the twelfth day. Easter was thirty-three days away, and that seemed like a terribly long time and a terribly long walk ahead of me. As the afternoon stretched out, I had lost sight of the earlier consolations.

I felt tired and depressed. All I wanted was to have a comfortable place to stay and do some laundry and take a bath. I did not want to go begging. I had done it last night and the night before. I wanted a break.

Then I remembered the seminary. The archdiocese of Los Angeles had a seminary in Camarillo, just outside Somis. But it was two miles out of my way and up in the hills. Should I go there? No, that was a temptation, an escape hatch from the most fundamental effect of real poverty: its inescapability. So I decided to beg, like it or not.

A voice within me asked, "Have I ever let you down?"

"No," I answered.

"Then what makes you think I will now?"

I felt sheepish. And reassured. Still I did not want to go through the insecurity and the refusals until someone took me in. Besides, this was farm country and dwellings were scarce. Just miles of lemon and orange groves. I asked the Lord to somehow make it easy. I was too weary and depressed to face a prolonged search for hospitality.

Ahead on the right was a large white house. Since it was the only one in sight, it was the logical place to start. A young man answered the door. He looked Mexican. I told my story.

"This isn't my house. You'll have to speak to my mother," he said, opening the door wider to reveal a middle-aged Mexican woman standing at the top of the stairs. I looked up to greet her, but before I could begin to retell my story, she said, "I think that will be all right. Come in. My husband won't mind."

I could not believe my ears. The inner whisper repeated, "Have I ever let you down?"

The mother's name was Bertha, and her son was Orlando. They showed me into an elegant sunken living room with plush sofas on three sides of a large square coffee table. For a while I was left alone to rest and write in my journal. Then I helped Orlando type a drama report for college. Bertha cooked enchiladas and rice for dinner.

While I was on the phone to Berkeley, Bertha's husband Al and her teenage daughter Lorie arrived home. Al was a barber in Saticoy, the next town on my route. He was swarthy, with short, close-cropped black hair, short of stature and medium build. He was an aggressive conversationalist, but not threatening, a quality that one looks for in a good barber.

During dinner Al asked what sorts of people had taken me in so far. I told about some of them, concluding with the story of Rick and his front porch light. Al got a faraway look, as if he had just been put in touch with some belief or ideal that had become clouded. Perhaps he had been losing faith in the goodness of people. Whatever it was, I knew at that moment that I had been led to this house for a reason.

Al broke the silence by saying he was "on the greasy chute" in the eyes of the church. He was being unfair to himself, I thought. Earlier he had told me about his faith and his prayer. They were unsophisticated, but sincere and direct. I had no doubt that this man was close to God.

"Al," I pointed out, "some regular churchgoers have turned me away, but you've accepted me into your home."

"You can't blame them, though," he objected.

"I don't," I assured him. "But there are many roads to God, and who can say that you aren't on one of them?"

The conversation shifted. I hoped he would think about our exchange.

At about 9:00 P.M. I retired to the playroom, where a bed had been prepared for me. There I celebrated Mass alone. Knowing that I would occasionally be away from formal places of worship, I had packed a small brass cup, a plastic bottle of wine, a few altar breads, and a missalette. The Eucharist is not meant to be a private devotion, nor do I like to celebrate alone. Yet the Mass is the culmination of all Christian experience, so I did not want a day to pass without it. I sat on the foot of the bed, a coffee table for my altar. The liturgy was simple and quiet. And when the Lord and I had become one in Communion, I slept.

Tuesday, March 13.

By 7:45 A.M. I was heading west on Route 118, a narrow, two-lane truck road with no sidewalk. The Southern Pacific tracks ran along my left. As far as I could see on both sides were lemon and orange groves almost ready for picking.

Walking was unpleasant. Light rain forced me to wear my poncho. Eastbound eighteen-wheelers nearly blew me into the groves every minute or two. I felt like the turtle on the road in the opening pages of *The Grapes of Wrath*. My glasses were so splattered that when I cleaned them I was surprised to find it had stopped raining.

At 11:45 I stuck my head into Al's barber shop in Saticoy for a final thank-you. Around the corner I picked up Telephone Road, a straight shot of about nine miles southwest into Ventura. Clouds and mist prevented me from seeing the Pacific, though I craned my neck longingly during the last few miles. I had been inland for a week.

Despite the weather and trucks, prayer was easy and consoling that day. I experienced a prolonged reverie of union with Jesus. I improvised songs to my beloved, extolling him as my all, my life, and my love, the one who walks, breathes, and loves in me.

Being a male in modern America, I feel a bit awkward writing about Jesus as "my beloved." At the same time I am convinced that that is a hangup I would be happier without. Male Christian mystics of the past used romantic language freely, and were richer for it.

Mission San Buenaventura is on Main Street in downtown Ventura. A 110-year-old Norfolk pine dwarfs the church's bell tower and serves as the primary landmark.

The mission was the ninth and last one founded by Fr. Serra. Most of the original structure is gone now. There is no enclosed courtyard as in the original days, nor are there the long arched walkways. The mission church has been suitably restored, and in a religious goods shop nearby is a museum displaying one of the finest collections of mission artifacts.

San Buenaventura was administered by a monsignor—an archivist for the Los Angeles archdiocese and an accomplished historian of the missions. I had been anticipating meeting him, eager to flesh out my skeletal knowledge of some mission history. On the day of my visit the mission rectory was full, so the monsignor arranged for me to spend the night at Assumption Rectory a few miles away. He also invited me to concelebrate at the 7:30 Mass the next morning, even getting me rides between the two parishes. This meant that we would have hardly any time for conversation. In the five minutes we had together, the pastor showed interest in my undertaking and asked me to send him an account of it. Hearing that I was walking without funds, he remarked, "Well, we'll have to do something about that."

I made a private tour of the mission church and museum, stopping to deposit $9.00 into the poorbox. When one of the assistant priests showed up to drive me to Assumption Parish, he handed me a white envelope from the pastor. It contained $10.00. As fast as I gave money away, it returned.

I celebrated Mass at 5:00 for a small community of Franciscan brothers who lived next to Assumption Rectory, then ate dinner with the staff of the parish.

When the meal was over, I was subjected to a reprimand in the kitchen. The pastor introduced me to Rosie, the young cook, and to Moe, the housekeeper. Moe was an older woman and not a Catholic. When she heard about my pilgrimage, she unhesitatingly challenged me: "If you're a priest, then why aren't you in church saying

Masses for people?" I tried to explain that ministry had many facets, but I did not get very far. Moe's mind was made up.

The evening was quiet. I took a bath and did laundry. My toe blister had filled with fluid again. I was still concerned about infection, but decided to wait it out.

That night I spoke to Ed in Berkeley for the last time. He was to fly to Rome to teach at the Gregorian until after Easter. Together we reflected on some trends of the pilgrimage. The experience of begging had changed. At first it had been frightening. Then success had made it gratifying and even a bit of an adventure. Now that both the fear and novelty were wearing off, I was beginning to feel impatient. I was getting tired of not knowing where I would sleep the next night. The spiritual and psychological effects of the long haul were beginning to show. Ed and I agreed that it was a good sign, but Ed wondered if I should take a day off to rest at Santa Barbara. After all, I had been going almost two weeks without a break. I was loath to do that, though. I still had Sonoma as a goal, still oriented toward achievement. I promised Ed I would think about resting and would stop if I felt I needed to.

Later I did reflect on Ed's suggestion. I concluded that the momentum I had going was important and that I should only rest if it were absolutely necessary to keep my spirit or body from breaking. At present my body was fine, I thought, and my spirit was just beginning to undergo some important and subtle changes. The monotony and loneliness of walking were having a positive effect. I prayed for an increase of patience and for fuller surrender to the Lord's will and providence. I prayed also for a softening of my inner rigidity and a shift toward a more easygoing approach to life. Finally I asked that I let all my feelings come to the surface, rather than subconsciously editing out the ones I judged inappropriate for a man of God, as was my habit. It was unfair to both God and myself to decide *a priori* that there would be certain ways in which

God could not speak to me. To restrict God's freedom is proportionately to restrict one's own.

Wednesday, March 14.

This day was to mark the end of what I now call my initiation as a pilgrim. The first two weeks were remarkably parallel to the "First Week" of the Spiritual Exercises. Like the opening phase of the retreat, these days constituted a period of purgation, of discovering and repudiating my sinfulness. They marked dramatic liberation from habits and attachments that held me back from interior advancement.

Each of the four sections of the journey unfolded spiritual trends proper to the corresponding "weeks" of the Ignatian retreat. On this fourteenth day I was to relinquish, at least partially, a major block to the rhythm of pilgrimage: my consuming preoccupation with reaching a goal on schedule.

I rose at 6:00 A.M. tired and disturbed, having slept fitfully. I had been awakened periodically by leg pains and by a vague fear of oversleeping and missing my ride to the mission.

Something in me said it was going to be a hard day. One concern was my blister. It had refused to dry up and appeared to have pus in it. I considered going to a clinic or an emergency room, but rejected that idea because it meant I would lose half a day waiting to be treated. Instead I simply asked God to take care of it. I do not know, at this point, whether or not I believed he would.

At 7:00 a green VW bug pulled up in front of Assumption Church to take me to the mission for Mass. The driver was an old Mexican cobbler named Juan, a mellow gentleman with gray hair, craggy face, and large, warm eyes. He was a regular communicant at the morning liturgy. Juan asked me how my feet were and if I had any blisters. I told him about my toe. Warning me of the danger of pus, he told me to lance it with a needle and drain it. Then I was to draw a piece of thread through it with the needle, snipping off the needle and leaving the thread in for a couple of days. The thread would act as a siphon, keeping the blister open and draining. I had never heard of that folk remedy before, but after breakfast I performed the operation. The fluid that had formed was clear, so I was ahead of any infection. Two days later the blister was dry and healing.

After Mass and breakfast at the mission, I turned down East Main Street toward the Pacific. The morning was sunny and warm. My destination was Carpinteria, twenty miles up the coast, sixteen miles short of Mission Santa Barbara, and only six miles short of the Jesuit novitiate at Montecito, the site of my thirty-day retreat.

Again I was following the Pacific Coast Bicycle Route, heading almost due west and a little north. Below on my left was the railroad, then the sea. Above on my right was the freeway, then sheer hills rising to the sky. The hills cascaded down toward me with steep canyons carved out by rain and earthquakes. Some were grassy; others were faced with bare, reddish-brown sandstone. My entire day was to be spent along this narrow, flat shelf, sometimes only seventy-five yards wide, between the hills and the ocean. If I had been feeling more alert and energetic, the walk would have been one of the most beautiful of the whole pilgrimage. In my fatigue, I felt only confined by the shelf and anxious to be finished.

The bike path dropped down to the shore and met old Route 101 again. I sat and watched the surf, but could not pray.

For about two hours I kept time with a railroad repair train. It would overtake me, then stop ahead to work on the track. I would pass it and tramp on, then it would overtake me again. The day was so tedious that such a distraction was a blessing.

By noon I was dazed. I went down to a small county park on my left to rest and eat. What I really wanted was sleep. After nibbling on part of my lunch at a picnic table, I sat on the ground with a thick log at my back and dozed. After only a few minutes, my need to reach Carpinteria roused me, and I trudged on. Partially because of my poor night's sleep, but mainly because of two weeks of non-stop exertion, I was plodding along half-conscious. Prayer was still impossible.

The sky ahead was changing. Billowy black clouds swirled down from the hills threatening rain. The weather seemed to be sympathizing with my mood.

Stopping on a rise to admire the sea, I noticed some slightly weathered magazine pages strewn at my feet. I turned a couple over with the butt of my staff. They were color photographs from something like *Playboy* or *Penthouse*. I picked up a few of them for a closer look. They were good. Almost immediately they began to have their intended effect. I was beginning to loosen the reins on something in myself that was inconsistent with who I wanted to be. I dropped the pages, not without hesitation and regret. Weakened by loneliness and fatigue, I would have loved to indulge my fantasies and my body. Ambling away I reflected wryly that the devil was even here in my desert. It did not surprise me, though, because that was where Jesus had met him. The monastic Fathers had not settled in the desert to escape the enemy, but to resist him with greater fortitude and constancy.

At about 3:00 P.M. I ascended a final grade into Santa Barbara County and the outskirts of Carpinteria. From there I could see a few miles ahead, thick with dark clouds, the familiar jagged profiles of the Santa Ynez Mountains falling toward the sea. Among them loomed Trinity Mountain. That was my own name for it. It was a high mountain with a wide, flat ridge. A pair of canyons divided its steep, grassy face into three equal cascades. Towering over my Long Retreat the preceding September, the mountain had become for me a symbol of the constant and unconquerable Trinity. I strained to see that mountain among the black clouds. When it came into view I felt closer to God and to myself than I had all day.

Since it was still early, I decided to move on to the northwest end of town before looking for lodging. That would put me a couple of miles closer to Santa Barbara, shortening the next day's walk. The clouds were clearing away. As I walked west, I could see Trinity Mountain clearly. That was the first temptation. Skip Carpinteria and go to the novitiate. I had friends there, Jesuit priests and novices I had gotten to know in September. I had not seen a Jesuit in two weeks. I had not seen a single familiar face in two weeks. Every day I was meeting strangers, reintroducing myself and re-explaining my purposes. A stranger in a strange land. I wanted a break. I *needed* a break. I would be treated well at the novitiate. I would be fed and bedded in a Jesuit house. I would be understood, perhaps admired. The novices would make a fuss over me. My vanity wanted that. But it was a temptation. I had to stay in Carpinteria. Besides, I had contracted with Ed that I would not go to a Jesuit house unless I had to. There, it was settled.

A mile later I came to a row of small, poor houses. Here was my chance to act against the prejudices I had felt on Beach Boulevard a week earlier. I went door-to-door giving my usual speech.

Some doors were not answered. At others I was told that the house was overly full already, or there was someone sick to take care of, or babies that should not be disturbed, or parents were not home, or just "No." At several houses I was advised to go the Catholic church, two miles back. Discouraged at the number of refusals, I decided to try the other side of the freeway.

On the overpass, I looked up at Trinity Mountain and had to quell the temptation again, this time with greater difficulty. Now in a more affluent part of town I rang the doorchimes of newer houses with manicured lawns, weed-less gardens, and two cars in the driveway. The same polite excuses.

One lady stands out in my memory because of the depth of her compassion. She had a sick father-in-law to tend. She hesitated so long her eyes began to get watery. "I really hate to send you away," she said, with pain in her voice. Through the screen door I tried to console her. "It's all right. Really. I understand. Don't worry about me. I'll get a place. Really. And . . . thank you." That woman's conflict over having to say "no" taught me to respect what went on inside other people who turned me away. Though they did not show it visibly, their struggle could have been just as trying as hers. I began to pray for them just as I prayed for those who opened their homes to me.

After several more houses my endurance was wearing thin, and between rejections I caught myself casting long-ing glances toward my Mountain. It was drawing me toward itself with increasing magnetism. The truly poor person, however, has no "back up," no "easy out" from his poverty. Perhaps there would come a day when I would not, either. But this time I did. "To hell with it," I thought. I had fought the fight. I had honestly done my part, I told myself. What seemed a temptation now held the aspect of a call from the Lord. Fatigue, desolation, and the long row of refusals—all conspired to move me toward the novitiate. Convinced it was right, or not caring if it were wrong, I sprang toward Montecito.

What seemed at the time momentous and complex appears now almost ludicrous. Why in the name of heaven did I so vigorously resist the decision to visit the novitiate? On the psychological level it came from my rigidity, per-fectionism, and orientation toward achievement. I had decided beforehand that to be an authentic pilgrim I would have to avoid all contact with familiar people and places. That was a condition for holiness which I had laid on myself, not bothering to ask whether it came from the

Lord. If I did not meet that obligation, I would be a failure, or at least imperfect and less holy.

But why had I taken such a rigorist or purist position from the outset? A Jesuit psychiatrist gave me a clue during a workshop at the tertianship several weeks after my return. When in the course of a group discussion I mentioned that I had been orphaned as an infant and adopted over a year later, he saw a possible motive for the pilgrimage. "Doesn't it make sense," he asked, "that such an early experience of abandonment and such a hiatus in nurturance could inspire you to go out alone into the world to prove that you could make it, to prove that rejection today has not the power over you that it had in your infancy?" If that conjecture is more accurate than not, it could explain, at least in part, why I stood so adamantly on a principle that was so arbitrary.

On a deeper spiritual level the problem pivoted on my restricted notion of divine call. I felt "called" to be a pilgrim. In living that out I operated as if God were outside myself revealing, step by step, a master plan that I was bound to follow if I wished to remain faithful. In such a model God appeals to the mind. The aforementioned obligation was in my head. A more helpful spirituality of call would be lodged in the heart. God's love dwelling within me moves me to make free and spontaneous choices that are congruent with salvation and growth in holiness. The point at which psychology and spirituality come together in all of this is belief in God's oneness with the human, which is what the incarnation and grace are all about. Result: the inspired leap into the abyss of self-trust.

Like an elastic stretched to the limit and suddenly released, I shot toward Montecito with manic determination, covering six miles in an hour and a quarter. I craved familiar faces and a place I could identify as "home." To my discredit, I was further spurred by a vain desire to make my entrance while the community was gathered at dinner.

Once I accepted the decision to stop at the novitiate, the second decision came easily. I really did need a day off to rest, even more than I needed to achieve the goal of Sonoma. Listening at last to God speaking through my body, I decided to ask for a second night's hospitality at Montecito.

When I staggered into the dining hall red-faced and panting from my forced march, I was surprised to find hardly anyone home. The novices and most of the staff were away on formation experiments, leaving only a couple of priests and a brother to mind the store. No danger here of my vanity feeding on too many strokes.

The administrator of the house gave me food and a room, readily granting my request to stay an extra day. The instability of being homeless had taken a heavy toll on my psyche, causing considerable mental fatigue. It was a luxury to know for the first time in two weeks where I would sleep for two nights consecutively.

Thursday, March 15: Day of Rest

It was a misty day with periods of rain. In a sluggish daze I whiled away the hours with long naps, light reading, and proximate reflecting on this opening phase of the journey.

During the first two weeks the Lord had initiated me into the ways of the wilderness. It had been a period of challenges, discoveries, and realizations. Patterns and rhythms of walking and praying had emerged. My legs and spirit had gained new strength by passing through pain. The first romantic fervor had worn off. Loneliness had become a force to be reckoned with. Poverty had been both a burden and a liberation. Begging had moved through crisis to become an accepted way of proceeding. And all along I was growing in self-understanding and intimacy with God. As with Hosea, the Lord had led me into the desert and spoken to my heart, sometimes gently, sometimes roughly, but always lovingly.

II

"I Look to the Mountains"
Ps 121:1

Montecito to San Luis Obispo
March 16–23, 1979

0 10 25

Miles

Mission San Luis Obispo

Arroyo Grande

Orcutt

Mission La Purisima Concepcion

Mission Santa Ines

Cachuma Village

Mission Santa Barbara

Montecito

Ventura

Friday, March 16.

Before leaving the novitiate, I lolled in the spring sun for an hour with Joe, my Jesuit friend who had introduced me to the mission chain the previous September. He was my age, gentle and joyful, sensitive and soft-spoken. Though our acquaintance was recent, our rapport was rare and easy, allowing us to muse intimately about our desires and fears.

What had started as a lazy chat turned gradually into a pensive sharing. My companion was facing a serious decision which, he said, if he could make it, "would be like staring down some huge monster. I could face anything in the future." He felt both eager and unready.

Noticing a similarity with my own recent wrestlings, I cautioned that our choices are best made in the Lord's time. "There are some monsters he just doesn't want us to stare down right now. King Lear was right: 'Ripeness is all.' It's like pilgrimage. There are times when the flat road is better than the mountain road, even if it's more roundabout. It can save your strength for the day when the mountain road is the only one. You have to consider what will serve the Lord best in the long haul."

Why I was so zealous in giving Joe permission to delay his decision is unclear. Perhaps I was attempting to satisfy my own need for greater flexibility. Whatever the reason,

I know that any observant pastoral supervisor would have done a number on me for being so directive.

I was on the road again at 10:00 A.M. With only ten miles to walk, and with delightful weather, it would be like a second rest day. My route was a country road about a mile inland, lined with trees, sprawling ranch-style homes, riding stables, and a swank country club.

Idling in Montecito had been wise, despite my fretting over the decision. I had awakened at six o'clock physically restored, mentally fresh, and emotionally optimistic. One dark cloud lingered, however. These next two weeks would take me through barren hill country. If I could make it to Carmel safe and healthy, the remainder of the walk would be gravy. In the meantime I would be feeling more keenly my need for the Lord.

Departing the novitiate and heading into sparsely populated mountains reminded me of pilgrims in the Old Testament preparing to leave the safety of Jerusalem after their visit to the holy temple. The hilly terrain of Judaea confronted them with their vulnerability, and their prayer became Psalm 121:

I lift up my eyes toward the mountains.
    Whence shall help come to me?
My help is from the Lord
    who made heaven and earth.

May he not suffer your foot to slip;
    may he slumber not who guards you.
Indeed he neither slumbers nor sleeps,
    the guardian of Israel.

The Lord is your guardian; the Lord is your shade;
    he is beside you at your right hand.
The sun shall not harm you by day,
    nor the moon by night.

The Lord will guard you from all evil;
    he will guard your life.
The Lord will guard your coming and your going,
    both now and forever. (NAB)

By two o'clock the Alameda had twisted over foot-hills, through valleys, and down to the coastal shelf again, depositing me before the massive facade of the Queen of the Missions, Santa Barbara.

After a wait of over an hour, I caught the superior of the Franciscan community, Father Virgil, on the fly between appointments. He found me a room in the loft over the arcade that formed the front of the monastery. Brother Sam, the community handyman, helped me make the bed and showed me around the friary. He seemed to be in his early forties, warm, hospitable, and simple. I liked him right away. He struck me as what Francis looked for in his *fratelli*.

At dinner I was befriended by four Franciscan pastors from Louisiana who were in Santa Barbara for a month of theological retooling. They took a shine to me and were fascinated by what I was doing. Their interest and affirmation bolstered my spirits, which had begun to sag under the weight of a continuous heavy rain. I knew the Lord was again sending me support and encouragement. But all the way from Louisiana?

That night I had trouble dropping off to sleep. The pelting rain on my window gave no promise of stopping. Morning would confront me with the San Marcos grade and the beginning of wilderness. My two archfears, cold and rattlesnakes, swirled in my head. Against cold I was powerless, except for begging. Against snakes I could take precautions. Rising from bed, I retrieved my little snake-bite kit from the bottom of my pack and studied the directions. When I felt familiar with the kit, capable of using it quickly and effectively, I was able to sleep.

Saturday, March 17: St. Patrick's Day

The rain had stopped, leaving the morning air clear and brisk. Standing at the base of the San Marcos grade, eight miles of winding road rising over two thousand feet, I could see the pubs of South Boston adorned with shamrocks and leprechauns. They looked mighty appealing. "What am I doing here?"

I attacked the grade with vigor, soon becoming winded and forced to slow down. Prayer was non-verbal, directed mainly at the business of climbing. The narrow snaking road with its frequent blind curves sharpened my watchfulness for what little traffic did approach.

Exertion was counterpointed by panoramic beauty on all sides. Ahead and to my right were the peaks and ridges of the Santa Ynez Mountains with vast falling walls of rock or not-so-sheer slopes of tree-dotted brush lands. Behind and to my left dropped an arresting display. From a height equivalent to that of a 180-story building I looked down tree-lined canyons and ravines that sloped to grasslands and eventually planed off to the coastal shelf of Goleta and Santa Barbara. Beyond lay the Pacific, deep blue in the morning sun. Farthest away the horizon was broken by the Channel Islands, Santa Cruz and Santa Rosa, veiled in thin blue mystery. Each time I paused to look, I wanted to linger and admire. It was an effort to turn away and continue to climb.

The ascent itself was no mean feat. Despite my moderate pace and liberal rest stops, I was flushed and perspiring long before I crested the pass. I had to ration my water because I had no idea where the next refill would come from. No accessible houses were evident.

As the climb got longer, my pack got heavier. I became conscious of Jesus carrying his cross. I could imagine its weight as my pack straps pulled at my shoulders, and I could identify with the Lord's staggering and fatigue.

The road began to level off and I thought I was near the top. Then a yellow warning sign came into view: "Hill. Trucks use lower gears next 4 miles." For a moment I missed the point and dreaded four more miles of climbing. Then I caught on. "Hill" meant "down." I had conquered the grade.

Panting and exultant, I turned into a side road where a summit lodge invited me to rest and fill my water bottle. Flopping into an overstuffed chair beside an unlighted pot-belly stove, I stared straight ahead into a whole wall of glass-doored refrigerators full of beer. How good a beer would have tasted at that moment. And how poor I felt with only my two dimes. Instead I had to be satisfied with lukewarm water.

The inhabitants of this stopover were the typical, counter-cultural mountain folk who free-wheel in the upper realms: bushy-bearded men in lumberjack outfits and emaciated, straggly-haired, baby-toting young women in long rawhide skirts. It was too stereotyped to be staged, so I concluded it was real.

A girl behind the deli counter let me fill my bottle from a tumbler of distilled water. Before leaving I tightened my boot laces, remembering that the salesman had warned me against the danger of downhill slippage.

The road down was wider and straighter, turning left to hug the north side of the mountains and dropping almost fifteen hundred feet to the floor of the Santa Ynez River valley and Lake Cachuma.

Across the valley, about twelve miles away, the glistening San Rafael Range bobbed up in receding rows of increasing height, culminating in the Sierra Madres twenty-five miles away. They radiated colorfully in the high sun: blue, purple, and every imaginable shade of green. The two highest peaks of the near range, McKinley and San Rafael, were capped with white from the previous night's storm. Almost mesmerized by the view, it took me several minutes to begin to resent the strong, cold headwind that was opposing me. If I had been climbing rather than descending, it would have been deadly. As it was, I came down with such determination that I was heedless of possible damage to my shins and ankles. Only when they began to hurt did I exercise restraint. Carelessness on the downslopes can cause more severe long-range problems than exertion on steep upgrades. I was to learn that lesson the hard way during the next few days.

The floor of the valley lay seven hundred feet above sea level, putting fifteen-hundred-foot mountains to my immediate left. The sun would fall behind them early in the day, bringing chill and darkness sooner. I watched Lake Cachuma grow larger and rise up to meet me, wondering apprehensively if I might find lodging along her shores. In an attempt to beat back the specter of dread, I began to sing:

Only in God will my soul be at rest:
From Him comes my hope, my salvation. . . .
God Himself is a refuge for us
And a stronghold for our fear.[5]

Four hours later, having gained the far end of the lake without seeing a trace of civilization, and with concern mounting, I came upon two signs. The first located me. "Solvang, 14 mi.; Santa Barbara, 24 mi." I could quit for the night wherever I found a place. The second sign gave me immediate hope. "Riding Stables: One Mile." That meant people.

Cachuma Trails Riding Stables were less than glamorous: two split-rail corrals, a couple of aging horse trailers, a pick-up truck, and an oversized house-trailer painted pink. Across the mudflat that constituted the center of operations a slender young woman in jeans, denim jacket, and peaked work cap saw me at the trailer door and started toward me. Blonde hair flowed out from under the cap. The closer she approached, the prettier she looked. I met her half way.

Having established that she was in charge, I told my story and asked for protection from the elements. She was understanding, but had no place to put me. To prove her sincerity and give me a second chance, she called her husband over and explained my situation. He confirmed that they really had no place for me. I knew they were telling the truth. The woman offered to drive me to the mission in Solvang, but I demurred. Then she suggested "the village" a mile and a half ahead, offering to drive me there. The sun was so low and I was so tired that I accepted. Good thing, too. I would never have found it.

The pickup turned onto an unmarked side road. A few hundred yards into the trees the road dipped down and opened out to an oval-shaped circle of twenty-three small white houses. No stores; no gas station; no church, school, or post office. Just those little white houses huddled in a circle in the shadow of the Cachuma Dam, completely hidden from the main road.

"Here we are. Cachuma Village," announced my driver. I still did not know her name. "You should find someone here who'll take you in. They're mostly retired folks. Just tell them Ted and Jane brought you in and vouch for you. They all know us here. Good luck."

At the first house company was coming. The woman pointed to a lady walking in the yard of the second house: "Try her."

I tried her. She was going out. "But try that house with the brick chimney down the other end. She has a back room."

Instead of going all the way down, I went to the third house. Full up. All females, adults and children. And guests were coming. One of the little girls pointed across the oval at a house with a camping trailer in the driveway: "Try there. Maybe he'll let you sleep in his trailer."

That sounded plausible. I walked across and rang the bell. A very thin, older man with red hair and moustache and a red two-day beard answered the door. I told my story and he invited me in to check with his wife. She was about the same age as the man, with light blonde hair, and very thin like her husband. She handed the decision back to him, and he said yes.

Five people were in the house when I came on the scene: Barney, his wife, whose name I never heard, their five-year-old son Billy, and Robbie, their nine-month-old grandson who stayed with them while their daughter rode with her trucker husband. The fifth person in the house was Rusty, the woman outside the second house who had told me to go "down the other end." Rusty did not speak to me, but a couple of minutes after I sat down she called Barney into a back room for a pow-wow. Something inside told me she was trying to convince him to get rid of me. I prayed like crazy, scanning the living room for a religious symbol that might give me some assurance. There was none. The conference seemed interminable. When finally they emerged, Barney offered me a cup of coffee. Not a word was said about their negotiations. I breathed deeply and took off my boots. Rusty left.

The coffee had a restorative effect. Altitude and headwinds had chilled me through. I felt awkward and humbled when Barney's wife set before me salad and reheated spaghetti from their meager dinner. Of the little they had, they gave. The lines on their faces told me that theirs had not been an easy life.

These were private people. We talked sparingly, and I respected their desire for silence.

Alone in the unheated trailer, I supplemented Barney's sleeping bag with a heavy blanket, then wrote in my journal till my fingers began to stiffen. Frigid night air had seeped quickly into my camper.

Suddenly the lights went out. Barney, thinking I had retired, had cut the electric umbilical that linked the trailer to the house. I groped my way into the sleeping bag fully clothed, including sweater, jacket, watchcap, and double socks. Zipping the bag all the way up around myself, I created a cocoon with only a small air hole near my nose. Had I been forced to stay outside, I would probably have caught a severe chill, possibly ending the walk.

Sunday, March 18.

The half-light of dawn and the chill penetrating my cocoon nudged me from my fetal huddle. Breakfast was an apple. I slipped quietly away from Barney's trailer and Cachuma Village. It was a gray day, and I felt gray. Having crawled through the night just beneath the surface of sleep, I set out in a semi-daze and wakened slowly as I walked. The road and valley were mine, free of traffic. The stillness of deep prayer raised my heart, stripping away all but the center of trust. The Lord was there. Looking within I found beauty that surpassed the wide valley and low mountains.

My reverie was jostled only once. A highway patrolman stopped to ask if I had broken down or was just hiking. His easy manner let me slip back into prayer as soon as he was gone.

Though I had covered only ten miles, I entered the town of Solvang limping. My left shin needed favoring. I had come down from San Marcos too fast.

Solvang is a Danish enclave that has decided to capitalize on the fact. Tourism reigns. Facades are Danish, along with pastries, glassware, woodwork, and delicatessens. There is even a windmill. One monument, however, stands against all of this, silently reminding Solvang of her true Spanish and Indian roots: Mission Santa Ines.

I reached the mission at 10:30 A.M., in plenty of time for the 11:00 and 12:30 Masses. A short, soft-spoken, gray-haired Capuchin Franciscan named Fr. Cyril received me at the back of the church. Though busy between Masses, he assured me of a place to stay and invited me to concelebrate with him at 12:30. He mentioned that no supper was served in the friary on Sundays, but added that I would "be taken care of." Then he disappeared into the mission, leaving me to my own resources for the next two hours.

I still felt fatigued from yesterday's marathon and my poor night's sleep, so I decided to just stay in the church until 12:30. If Fr. Cyril had not departed so quickly, I would have asked to be shown to a room where I could nap.

After the 11:00 Mass I stepped outside for fresh air and almost collided with Fr. Lambert, one of the Louisiana Franciscans who had befriended me in Santa Barbara. Right behind him were the other three. "We've come to take you out to lunch," he announced. After weeks of asking strangers for food and shelter, never knowing whether I would get what I needed, here were four men who had driven thirty-five miles to share a meal with me. I was deeply touched.

Later in the afternoon Lambert reached into my heart a second time by resurrecting a quaint old custom. As the friars were leaving he asked for my blessing. I gave it, feeling humbled and unworthy, then asked for his. In a ritualized way, we were saying how we felt about each other.

It was almost three o'clock when I was shown to my room by Brother Patrick, the other half of the Santa Ines Capuchin community. He was a native Irishman, very old and thin, with snow white hair and beard. Like Fr. Cyril, he was soft-spoken and simple. He had served the Lord on his knees and with his hands for many years, and he was so practiced in humility that he seemed not to give it a thought. He acted spontaneously and it came out humble. When we met for the first time, he took my right hand in both of his and kissed it. I was embarrassed, but to him it was the natural thing to do.

Brother Patrick's brand of humility was really a distillation of wisdom and self-acceptance. He knew life. He knew God. And he knew himself. There was no doubt in his mind that God loved him unconditionally as he was. Owning that, he could love himself as he was. And then he did not have to wear a mask. He could act without constraint or artifice. If other people failed to understand, that was their loss. Brother Patrick's easy way, however, was a challenge to the inhibitions that keep the rest of us from showing ourselves to each other honestly.

I napped till five o'clock when Brother Patrick called me for dinner. He and Father Cyril were on their way out to visit a friend, so Brother served me a full-course steak dinner in the kitchen. It was twice my capacity. Three hours earlier I had eaten with the Louisiana friars. I was stuffed. Besides that, I was discovering that my stomach seemed to be shrinking. I had tightened my belt two inches in eighteen days. In addition, my eating habits were changing. I was satisfied with less food at any one time, preferring to eat small amounts more frequently. I judged that I was sufficiently nourished because I had the necessary energy for walking and praying. Unable to eat the whole meal, I wrapped some steak, potatoes, and carrots in aluminum foil and stowed them in my backpack for lunch the following day.

I spent the evening doing laundry, writing in my journal, and watching television. It was good to be alone, quiet, and warm. I was lulled to sleep by the steady patter of rain on the old mission roof, which I thanked God for putting over my head.

Monday, March 19: Feast of St. Joseph

Rain was still falling when I awakened, but by the end of Mass the sun was bright. The two Capuchins shared a

hot breakfast with me and sent me on my way with corned-
beef sandwiches.

My destination was Mission La Purisima Concepcion,
nineteen miles west on Route 246, then on to La Purisima
Church for the night, four miles south in the town of Lompoc. There are three one-day walks in the mission chain,
and this was to be my first. I could not stay overnight at
Purisima Mission because it was no longer an active religious facility. Two of the twenty-one missions, La Purisima
and San Francisco de Solano in Sonoma, are owned and
operated by the State of California as historical parks. My
plan was to stay at the rectories of their descendant parishes as the next best thing to lodging at the missions
themselves.

Visiting a mission that was a state park would be a new
experience. Would I be barred admission because of
inability to pay at the gate? It did not bother me. I could
talk my way in, or I could beg change from tourists. If the
Lord had brought me this far, he would get me in.

Broad hills and large granite outcroppings lay on both
sides, reminding me of God's firm and supportive love. For
some reason I thought of home and of how long I had been
away. A dark knot tightened in my chest and my eyes
misted. All the kindnesses of so many people had not filled
an essential gap: the need for a place to call "home." As
the only constant in my life, I turned to the Lord. "Only
you can be home for me now, Jesus. I must find my home
in you." Suddenly a song by Joe Wise expressed what I was
feeling:

> To be Your Body, to be Your Blood.
> How hard to learn, Lord, to die and live.
> To quick be broken, to heal again.
> To be Your Body, to be Your Blood.[6]

I sang it over and over, slowly, as a mantra, and entered
into communion with the Lord.

Dark clouds were forming ahead and blowing toward me. To my left, portions of hills were obscured by rainfall. I took out my army-green plastic poncho and carried it in my hand "just in case." Sure enough, within a few minutes drops were pelting the valley. I put on the poncho fast. My feet and legs were soaked, but my head, arms, torso, and pack were protected. Under the circumstances, I was in surprisingly good spirits, joyful even, walking with the Lord and feeling that there was no better place on earth for me to be than right here right now. My moods seemed to change as quickly as the weather.

The one problem with walking in the rain in the country is that there is scarcely a place to sit and rest. All the ground is wet, even under the trees. After some time, I figured I had covered seven or eight miles without a break. My boots were waterlogged and my jeans were sopping. Furthermore, I was getting hungry. So I started looking for a suitable shelter. The level valley floor had shifted to low rolling rises and depressions, limiting visibility. Ascending a long, low slope, I could see a white barn a few hundred yards ahead. I stepped up my pace.

While pressing toward the barn, I happened to look to my right. Nestled in the trees, almost unnoticeable because of its color and the rain, was a dull-green farmhouse. A tractor shed stood farther back. Because it was much closer than the white barn, I bolted across the road and down the driveway toward the shed. A tall, gray-haired, well-built man in work clothes was entering one of the shed's garages. I followed him.

"Hello. Do you mind if I come in out of the rain to rest and eat a sandwich?"

"No. Come in." He was immediately kind and welcoming. And he looked curiously familiar. He returned my stare with equal recognition. "I think I know you," he ventured. "I saw you in church yesterday."

"You did?" Things were beginning to click, but not completely.

111

"Yes. At the eleven o'clock Mass. You were down back."

Of course! It was Joe, the usher who had shown me to a rest room. I told him my name and explained that I was making a walking pilgrimage of the missions.

"You're not a priest, are you?"

"Yes, I am." My look of amazement amused him.

"I thought so yesterday. You knew the words to all the hymns, even the modern ones that the folk group sang that weren't in the missalette. And you sang them. I said to myself, 'That's a priest.'"

Joe took me into the house to meet his wife Kathy and their two small daughters. Things happened very quickly after that. Before I knew it, I had been invited for lunch, had changed to dry socks and jeans, my wet clothes were in the dryer, my boots were near a radiator, and my fingers were around a glass of wine. "Lunch" was a hot midday dinner.

On hearing that I was a Jesuit, Joe asked, "Do you know my nephew? He's a Jesuit studying at the theology school in Berkeley. He's my sister's son." I had indeed met Joe's nephew several times.

All through dinner and afterward, Joe kept pressing me to let him take me the rest of the way to Purisima Mission. I kept putting him off. The rain had stopped and sun was breaking through. Joe eventually wore me down, convincing me that I would get three of four miles out into nowhere and get drenched again. He knew the skies around there at that time of year. "Besides, you've lost so much time here you'll never make it to the mission before it closes." He should have been a politician.

Kathy gave me a gift for the road: Two large plastic garbage bags to wrap around my legs in future rains, and some rubber bands to keep them on.

Soon after our meal, Joe's friend Tim arrived with a pickup truck to cart Joe's motorbike into Lompoc for

112

repairs. A stop at the mission would not be out of their way at all.

It was about 2:15 when we reached the state park. My companions went into the tourist lodge with me, probably to cover me in case I had to pay admission. The lodge was empty. A sign on the counter said, "Ranger in Field— Please Pay Later." Seeing that I was in without a hitch, Joe and Tim said their farewells and drove away. I was alone again.

Because of the weather, the time of year, and the day of the week there was almost no one visiting the mission. I had the place virtually to myself. So the church ceased to be a tourist attraction and became a house of prayer. I knelt near the center of the altar rail and enjoyed the luxury of solitude in this shrine to Mary. Those moments were precious and intimate, reminding me of Ignatius' all-night vigil before Our Lady's altar at Montserrat, during which he divested himself of sword and armor and abandoned his life of wealth and nobility. The following morning he put on the beggar's garb of a pilgrim.

After praying in the church for a while, I completed my tour of the mission. Just as Joe had predicted, the rain returned. I decided to wait in the church until it stopped, then walk the four miles to Lompoc. By about 3:45 the rainfall had become soft and steady, with no promise of letting up. I wrapped my legs in Kathy's dark green garbage bags, threw on my poncho, and set out for town looking like something from the set of a 1940's horror movie. But I was dry.

When I reached La Purisima Parish, the rain having ceased, I sat on the steps of the old church across the street from the rectory and removed the poncho and plastic bags. I did not want the housekeeper to open the door and find a cheap Halloween spaceman.

None of the priests were home, but the cook told me that the associate pastor was in the new church next door preparing for the 5:30 Mass. I found the priest "preparing" for Mass by praying on a kneeler in the sanctuary. He was of medium height, with short brown hair and fair complexion. He looked under forty. A few minutes before 5:30 he rose and entered the sacristy. I followed him. Without a moment's hesitation he granted my requests to concelebrate and to spend the night at the rectory.

After a simple fare of soup and pizza, I phoned Berkeley to report my progress. Bad news awaited me. A letter had arrived from my provincial in Boston. At my request Bernie, Ed Malatesta's assistant, opened it and read it to me over the phone. An assignment that I had been expecting and had set my heart on was not available. On the contrary, there was a gap in the religious education department at the high school I had left. Would I be willing to return there to resume my former position for another year, since that was the most urgent need of the province that I could fulfill at the present time?

Because the Lord was so close during pilgrimage, my reactions were different from those I would have expected. Even before hearing the entire letter, I had passed through disbelief and disappointment, and was working on accepting this as the will of God.

Jesuit obedience is not a blind, mechanical execution of commands issued coldly by superiors who are unconcerned about the feelings and needs of the men they govern. The constitutions of our Order, written by St. Ignatius himself, bind us to make known to superiors our inner desires concerning apostolic assignments. God reveals his will through the spiritual movements within the individual Jesuit as well as through the needs of the Church and society. No superior worth his salt can make valid assignments without considering all the ways in which God can be speaking to him.

I knew that my provincial was fully aware of my beliefs and desires regarding my next assignment. We had discussed them more than once, and he had concurred that the work I was requesting would be good for me. Now he was asking me if I would be willing to put it on "hold" for another year. Alone in Lompoc, three thousand miles from my province, the only data available to me for my decision were my own interior movements and dispositions.

Almost immediately I began to feel strong consolation at the thought of letting go of my own desires in favor of serving the Lord where I was really needed. I felt genuinely free. Without hesitation I wrote to the provincial. Yes, I would be willing to go back to the high school for a year, if that was where he needed to assign me. It was more important to be doing what the Lord wanted than what I wanted.

When I finished writing the letter, I still had deep peace and joy. Later in the evening I began to experience the negative feelings attached to my decision: anger at what I thought was the unfairness of such an unexpected change; fear and suspicion that the "one year" would become four or five; disappointment that the work I desired had been within my grasp and was now temporarily lost; resentment at my provincial for seeming to think that the work I felt called to was not as urgent a need of the province, the Church, and society. As the evening passed, these feelings grew subtle and submerged, but they did not disappear. Tomorrow I would have to face the task of grieving.

Tuesday, March 20.

The eighteen miles from Lompoc to Orcutt were cold and desolate. Wilderness and dark clouds accented my churning anger and depression. Five miles out I had to traverse the steep, winding Harris Grade that links the Santa Ynez and the San Antonio Valleys. After a laborious climb my severe descent was aggravated by raw headwinds sweeping up from San Luis Obispo Bay. With the gusts complementing my inner turmoil, I ignored the dictates of caution. Gravity pulled me downward, and I did nothing to resist. In rapid succession my heels struck the slope, pitching me forward for the next step, almost out of control. My ankles and shins were being banged and stretched without mercy. I gave no heed. All I knew was that I did not want to be where I was, or even who I was.

When I reached the floor and slowed to an amble, the road seemed endless and defiant, prodding me to move along. Even the buzzards and owls and skittish cattle eyed me as an alien in their valley. And the iron wind continued to oppose.

Grasping at straws, I tried to find some peace and security in a familiar prayer-fantasy. I imagined myself in the company of Aslan, the lion Christ-figure from C.S. Lewis' *The Chronicles of Narnia.*[7] He was mighty and graceful, with a bushy golden mane. The smoothness and power of his steps, along with his silence and ease of movement, gave me momentary self-possession. He knew my story and calmly saw it all as part of the Father's plan of love. While I could not see my own destination, I could imagine him seeing it and offering assurance. That gave me solace.

It did not last long, however. The image faded and I trudged angrily on. Begging was out. My psychic energy was drained. When I reached Orcutt I would use the cash I had been given in Lompoc to get a cheap room. I just wanted to brood alone. The town came into view in the distance after what seemed like many hours. Another mile brought me to a gas station. I approached the attendant.

"Can you tell me where I might get an inexpensive room around here? A hotel or something?"

"Not in Orcutt. Only rooms are in Santa Maria, six miles up."

I could not manage that. My feet were hurting and my shins were beginning to throb. I gave up the rooming-house idea, but still could not bring myself to go door-to-door. I supposed if I absolutely had to, I would.

"Is there a Catholic church in Orcutt?" I asked the attendant.

"Up Clark about a mile."

Clark Avenue was the main street in front of the gas station. I plodded on. Beside the road was a plastic quart bottle with screw-cap. I picked it up and examined it. It was better than my own, so I kept it.

I must have cut a pretty image limping into town with my stick in one hand and a plastic bottle in the other, my backpack with straw hat slung atop it, and my navy watch-cap pulled down over my ears.

Coming within sight of a large stone church, I was struck with a pang of guilt over seeking easy shelter. I banished it easily, deferring to my emotional and physical pains and needs.

The rectory was just a private home, and a small one at that. I explained myself to a snowy-haired Josephite. He laughed at my request for lodging. "This is nothing but a rabbit hutch. There's no room here. But I'll tell you what. Go down to our novitiate on Patterson. They'll have room for you. It's about a ten minute walk."

It was more like twenty-five. Patterson Road, a long residential street, took me back in the direction I had come from. I was looking for #180, expecting an institutional building. Almost at the end of Patterson, with nothing in sight but a few more small private homes, I concluded cynically that the pastor had just been trying to get rid of me. Then I saw a mailbox with the number 180 and the inscription: "Josephite Fathers." It stood in front of a small single-story white house set back from the road and obscured by trees and shrubs.

No one answered the doorbell, so I rang again. Still no answer. I went to the side door at the kitchen. No answer. No one preparing supper. There was a car in the driveway.

"Should I wait? Maybe they're out for the whole evening."
My heart sank. The perfect ending of a perfect day.

I slowly shuffled back along Patterson, wondering what to do next. I remembered seeing a Marriage Encounter sticker on a white van about three-quarters of a mile back. Maybe I could go there. I had been Encountered in early February. Surely they would take in an Encountered priest.

Before that thought had a chance to ripen, a clean-cut young man jogged by. Dark-complexioned and black-haired, he wore white running shorts and a white T-shirt with the initials C.Y.C. on the back. "I'll bet he's a Josephite novice," I told myself. I turned around to watch where he was heading. Sure enough, he veered into the novitiate driveway. I fairly flew back after him. As soon as I identified myself and asked for lodging, he said, "Sure!"

The Josephites were warm and generous, receiving me with genuine affection. Their hospitality somewhat dissipated the heavy clouds that had been hanging over me, since my painful but necessary grieving had just about run its course. That course had been shortened by an ironic gift: the lonely route, the grade, the wind, the dark clouds, even the animal life—all the forces of nature—almost as if they could understand, had respected my need to mourn.

Wednesday, March 21.

The morning was cool with an overcast sky and happily no wind. Arroyo Grande was twenty-five miles ahead, all of it on Route 1 and most of it through fields and forests. My mood had improved, so I did not dread the wilderness.

On the outskirts of Orcutt a sheriff's patrol car pulled in front of me and stopped. The barrel of a shotgun stood erect behind the dashboard. My thoughts began to race. I had not broken any laws. Perhaps I looked suspicious walking away from the federal prison at Lompoc. Maybe Route 1 became a freeway and I would be forbidden to walk it. Whatever it was, I felt defensive. The patrolman was a good-looking young deputy in uniform, with short brown hair and a neat moustache. He stood medium height and was in trim condition. As he approached I sensed benevolence.

"Good morning, Officer."

"Good morning. I think I recognize you."

"You do?"

"Yes. Aren't you a priest? Didn't you say Mass in Lompoc the other night? Monday?"

"Yes, I did."

"I was in the congregation. I saw your hiking boots under the vestments and it struck me as odd. Then I recognized the same boots a minute ago."

At that Mass at La Purisima not a word had been said about my identity or the pilgrimage. His powers of observation were keen.

After a brief chat, the deputy seemed on the verge of leaving, when he said, "Don't go away," and darted to his car. He returned with a banana and a tangerine, probably his own lunch. "Here. You'll need these more than I will. They'll taste good along the road."

I was almost speechless. That officer will never fully appreciate how much he did for me that morning. His simple kindness carried me forward for hours.

My stride that day was purposeful, but not rushed. I was in consolation, which meant I was satisfied to be where I was. I was not anxious to be somewhere else. I was moving in rhythm with reality, not bucking it. "Contemplation," says a friend of mine who hosts a house of prayer, "is simply doing one thing at a time, being fully present to the moment." That was how I felt.

I made Guadalupe by noon and two hours later had ascended a mesa covered with tall eucalyptus trees. All

119

around the mesa were oil fields, and in the distance to my left I could see the flaming tops of wells. Farther on I got a good sighting of Pismo Beach, Shell Beach, and San Luis Obispo Bay, with mountains beyond falling sharply into the Pacific.

My shins were troubling me again, especially the left one. I favored it, using my stick as a cane. Progress was slow, and I was feeling the length of the day. I was not in bad spirits, but my consolation had faded. I was beginning to feel tempted to look for another parish. Convinced that this was not from the Lord, I shook it off.

On the north side of the mesa the view stopped me in my tracks. Hundreds of feet directly below, and reaching far to the north and west, was the rich black floor of a farming valley, partly green with rows of vegetables. Far to the north towered the Santa Lucia Mountains.

The road down from the mesa twisted steeply, further straining my shins and increasing my limp. In addition, I was feeling my usual anxiety about where I would stay and how I would muster the courage to beg from door to door again. But I was determined to do it.

On the valley floor, Route 1 turned west toward Oceano. I stayed north on Valley Road into Arroyo Grande. As soon as I entered the town, a row of houses on the left beckoned me. I fought off one last temptation to skip it, gritted my teeth, and hobbled up the walk to the first house. An Oriental woman answered. She spoke only one word: "Sorry."

Second house: no one home.

Third house: another Oriental woman, with her family around her. She sounded quite friendly: "We're expecting company. We'd love to have you, but we can't. I wish you had come earlier so we could have delayed our guests." As I was leaving I heard the lock snap on the door behind me.

The fourth house raised my hopes. It displayed the Christian fish symbol near the top of the door. A short woman in her twenties with a pleasant round face, fair complexion, glasses, and brown pigtails came to the door. She wore blue jeans and a red bandanna print shirt.

Pointing to the fish, I identified myself as a Christian, gave my name, and began to explain my pilgrimage. Before I had a chance to ask for lodging, the woman said, "Oh, why don't you come in for a cup of coffee?"

"Well, thank you. That's very kind of you. But what I really need is a place to sleep tonight—a cot or a sleeping bag or anything."

She hesitated a moment and, turning to a nearby sofa, said, "Shelley?" A man stirred from his nap. He had dark hair and a bushy black beard. The woman explained to him what I wanted, and they soon agreed that I could sleep in the garage in a sleeping bag.

"I'm Mary and this is my husband Shelley. I presume you're Catholic?"

"Yes, I'm a Catholic priest."

"Oh! Do you want to go to a Christian concert tonight?"

"Sure!"

My stay with this family was an extraordinary and impressive encounter with faith and generosity. The couple had two small children, Christopher, 6, and Crystal, 4. Both had been born on March 22, so this was the eve of their birthdays. Shelley worked as a mechanic at a BMW service garage in Arroyo Grande. Mary was earning her license as an occupational therapist. Her kitchen was chock full of craft materials for ceramics, basket-weaving, painting, and woodworking. Both Shelley and Mary were born-again Christians belonging to Calvary Church, a small fundamentalist congregation in Grover City. Their house was rife with religious symbols, such as a large, painted wooden cross over the fireplace. A small tape deck was playing contemporary gospel music. Mary and Shelley were poor, and they lived by their faith.

I soon found that we were not alone in the house. A tall, slender, soft-spoken woman named Pam was in one of the bedrooms. She was in her early twenties, an attractive blonde with fair complexion and large soft eyes. With her she had a two-year-old daughter, Sarah. Pam and Sarah had needed a place to stay, so Shelley had taken them in.

While Mary baked cookies to take to the concert, Shelley showed me his aquaria. He loved sea life. Two tanks of sea water held specimens he had brought back from Shell Beach. Because of his respect for life, Shelley would keep them only until they were too big for the tanks, then he would put them back into the Pacific.

Mary saw me limping around the house and asked what was wrong. I explained about the downgrades and the pains in my shins. "Shin splints," she diagnosed. "They can last a long time. Let's pray so they'll go away."

After a meager supper Mary, Pam, and I and the children left for the concert. We rode to church in a rattle-trap tin can of a car. "Church" was a converted, corrugated aluminum garage with carpeting and about fifty metal folding chairs. A strong bond of community pervaded the small assembly, without excluding strangers. I was quickly made to feel welcome.

The performance was by two bearded young men in casual clothes. They were from the high country of Colorado, but earlier had lived in Arroyo Grande. They called themselves "Bethlehem." The lead man sang and played western guitar and occasionally harmonica; the second played electric guitar and sang harmony. They performed fundamental folk and folk-rock gospel music. It was melodic, easily singable, and deeply spiritual. A real personal faith came out of the pair, animating the entire congregation into spirited song. It made much of our Catholic liturgical music seem stilted and contrived. These folks were singing because they felt it.

After coffee and cookies, we drove home to find Shelley reading his Bible. The sofa in the living room had been pulled out to reveal a hide-a-bed. At first I thought Shelley had changed his mind about my sleeping in the garage. Then I discovered that the sofa-bed was where he and Mary slept. They had given their own bedroom to Pam and Sarah. And still they were making room for an unexpected pilgrim.

The night was cold and so was the garage. Shelley *had* changed his mind. Two thick layers of foam matting were spread on the kitchen floor, then the old army sleeping bag. I had a warm and dreamless sleep.

Thursday, March 22.

At 6:00 A.M., gospel music bouncing in from the living room lured me from my unconsciousness. "Where am I?" I thought. "What am I doing on a kitchen floor?" Then I remembered.

Soon Mary was baking a birthday cake for Crystal and Christopher. While the children were dressing, Shelley brought down from a high cupboard two hand-crafted wooden bathtub boats. Each had a paddle-wheel at the stern driven by a rubber band. Shelley had made the boats identical, except that one was of slightly darker wood than the other. He asked Mary to gift wrap them, carefully pointing out that the darker was Crystal's and the lighter was Christopher's.

I marveled at Shelley's loving wisdom and how it incarnated the way the Father deals with us. The gifts had not been bought, but had been made by the father for his own children. He had not made two identical boats and then attached names to them or painted them. Rather he had crafted each one with a particular child in mind, so that, even though the boats were equal in size, shape, and performance, while working on the darker wood he was thinking of Crystal and while fashioning the lighter he was mindful of Chris. He was showing that he loved his children equally and fully, but distinctly. And he knew that the slight difference in color would be enough to keep the children aware of which gift was his or her own. They could be unique without any cause for jealousy. There was much to learn here.

A small stained-glass plaque stood on a front window sill. When I read it, I knew it was not there merely for decoration.

> I shall pass this way but once.
> If there is any good or kindness
> That I can do,
> Let me not defer it,
> For I shall not pass this way again.

My shin splints were still painful and causing me to limp. Mary spent some time praying over me for healing. I think her faith in the power of prayer was simpler and deeper than mine.

As I was about to set my face toward San Luis Obispo, Pam, who had no home for herself or her child, offered me money for the road ahead. Thanking her, I suggested that she give it to someone more needy than I.

My heart was full of gratitude as I hobbled out of Arroyo Grande, though sad that I would probably never again see Mary or Shelley or Pam. They had taught me so much about trusting the Lord and being satisfied with what little they had.

Two months later I received a letter from Mary with a different address on the envelope. The explanation was inside:

> . . . As for our family, the Father has blessed us abundantly, even as He has said to look neither to the right, nor to the left, nor to the things of this world, but to God for all abundance.
> We are in great trial and having much tribulation, but to God the glory for He is ministering to all our

needs even as Jesus promised in Matthew 6:31–34. And we, seeking first the peace of Jesus, have grace sufficient to stand.

Shelley has injured his back and cannot work for a while. He hurt it in March. God has provided food, both through miraculous works and through the social system. He has taught us through all our agonies to lean on Him only.

We are moving out of the house to live semi-nomadic lives in a tent. God has taught us not to store up treasures on earth, but to look to heavenly storehouses for riches. He has shown us the truth of clinging not to material things but to Him. The owners of the house must sell or go under, and we cannot buy it, and we cannot pay the rent because our income is so low. Praise God, that He is divorcing us from the corrupt and corruptible, materialistic things of this earth and clothing us in riches and fine raiment, preparing us, His Bride, for the marriage feast of the Lamb. . . .

. . . Our food stamps have been cut off, so we are again relying solely on God to provide. . . . Praise God for the communion of prayer. In prayer the Holy Spirit lifts up my soul in great intercession and for a while I am free. Oh, the sweet joy of talking with the Father and basking in His love. . . .

Mary's unquestioning trust in God confronted me with the fragility of my own.

The whole fifteen miles to San Luis Obispo was a struggle. Pain in my left shin forced me to overwork the other leg. By midday a sharp sting shot up from my right big toe with each step. Progress was discouragingly laborious. I decided that I would ask to spend the next day resting at the mission. Mary's prayers would have a better chance of working if I coupled them with prudence.

A few miles south of the city three dogs charged out from a house set back from the road. Their barking and snarling unnerved me and I tried to diffuse their aggression by ignoring them and dragging my staff behind me.

When one of them, with teeth showing, went after the back of my feet, I turned on them and brandished my staff in an attempt at taking the offensive. At that moment a middle-aged woman appeared on the porch. I yelled across the expansive yard, with no little irritation in my voice, "Ma'am, I'm just walking by and minding my own business and your dogs are trying to attack me. Would you please call them off?"

"What are you doing there? You shouldn't be walking the highway, anyway."

I couldn't believe my ears. She was trying to put the blame on me! "It's a public road. I have a right to walk here," I countered.

"Well, they're just protecting my property."

"Not from me, they're not. I'm a peaceable man."

She did call the dogs back and I limped away, having completely lost my composure and spirit of prayer. I was so jarred by the attack and so angry at the woman for trying to put me in the wrong that I spent the next fifteen minutes rehearsing the encounter and thinking of things I could or should have said. I fantasized myself making a speech about how I am a Christian pilgrim who wishes good for everyone and who would never willfully harm anyone or damage anyone's property. I told her how offensive her dogs were and how poorly they spoke of her attitude toward the rest of the human race. I concluded by pointing out that if she were less concerned about her property and more concerned about people who have no property, the world would be a better place.

Now I was on a roll. Resentment fed my imagination. I envisioned the woman calling the police and having me arrested on the false charge of attacking her dogs and threatening her safety. I defended myself in court by contrasting myself to this lady who hates the world so much she has three dogs to keep it out. If the judge chose to take her word against mine, he was free to do so, but it would be on his conscience because God knew I was innocent and desired only two things: the consolation and salvation of all people, and the freedom to move peacefully forward on my pilgrimage.

By the time I realized the comic self-righteousness of my fantasies, I had dissipated my anger over the incident. Then I began to feel ashamed that I had not been able to muster a more patient and Christ-like tone in speaking to the woman. I reinterpreted what had happened. Perhaps she was a good religious person, even a regular church-goer, who had been robbed or in some other way wounded by the world. She might have simply been reacting out of her own experience and fear. I remembered my own apprehension and excessive caution after being mugged a few years earlier. That helped me forgive her, even pity her and love her. It all boiled down to the social nature of sin. There is no such thing as private sin. We are all victims. Every sin makes the world a harder place to enact God's love.

My reception at Mission San Luis Obispo was the antithesis of my doggie affair. The parish priests gave me the bishop's suite and unhesitatingly agreed to my resting there the following day. One of them even offered to get me medical attention. A fire was raging in my left shin and a spike was driving through my right big toe. There was no way I could climb the fifteen-hundred-foot Cuesta Grade in this condition. I declined the doctor. All I needed was rest.

Though necessary, the decision to halt for a second day was a surrender of my will to God's. The achiever in me still pushed toward Sonoma.

Skirmishes with ambition punctuated the whole journey. On one hand I desired the inner freedom to follow the Spirit wherever it called me. That might mean slowing down and listening more to the Lord and to other people. On the other hand I strove to complete the mission trail, which was a bid for recognition based on my need to define my self-worth by achievement.

That conflict even contaminated my prayer. "I place the entire undertaking in your hands, Lord. Help me to do your will." In reality, I wanted God to will what I wanted, but was ashamed to admit that to God or to myself. When the prayer on my lips differs from the one in my heart, I believe that God pays attention to the true inner prayer, even if I am not conscious of what it is. Much of what is called "growth in prayer" is simply getting in touch with what I really want and accepting that as part of who I am.

Friday, March 23: Day of Rest

After the eight o'clock Mass, at which I presided and preached, there was a virtual parade of parishioners into the sacristy. Several women gave me money. A shoe store owner offered me a new pair of boots. A young woman invited me to a teen retreat starting that evening. Several older women pressed me into joining them for breakfast at a local restaurant. And one old man with a thick Italian accent took both of my hands in his and made a speech about his being part Indian and about the Indians first calling the Jesuits the White Fathers. He asserted that my being on the road with the Lord was a sure sign that I had the Spirit of God in me. Handing me six rolled-up one-dollar bills, he said, "This is not for you. You won't need it. The Lord will take care of you. This is for you to do good for someone else."

After the restaurant breakfast and much grandmotherly attention, I walked back to the mission wondering if I should just stop telling people what I was doing. The kudos were making me nervous. I decided that this was a temptation. "Let your light shine," Jesus had said. As long as I worked at purifying my heart and avoided currying admiration for myself, then the good that could be done by sharing the pilgrimage would far outweigh the danger of vanity.

On the church steps I ran into Colleen, the young woman who had invited me on the teen retreat. A senior in college and full of idealism, Colleen asked to hear more about my journey. We idled away the rest of the morning, conversing about desert experiences, vocational choices, Carlo Carretto's books, Aslan, and a variety of other cabbages and kings.

I was in a good mood all day. It was a pleasure not to be walking, and I felt secure in knowing I had a bed for the night.

In the evening the parish had Stations of the Cross followed by Benediction. During the Stations I experienced a premonition of hardships to come and had a strong sense of sharing the sufferings of Christ. I also sensed that my concept of prayer was still too narrow. Till then I had thought of pain as hindering prayer. If I could appreciate pain as communion in the cross of Christ, then I need not fear that future difficulties would separate me from the Lord. They could be occasions of deeper intimacy.

During Benediction I felt, as I had several times before, the Lord filling me and transforming me into a likeness of himself. If that sounds pretentious, it was balanced by my painful awareness of the catalog of obstacles I continually placed in the way of grace. Considering my willfulness, it struck me that even the desire to be transformed had to have been a gift from God.

III

"Though I Walk Through the Valley"
Ps 23:4

San Luis Obispo to Carmel
March 24–April 1, 1979

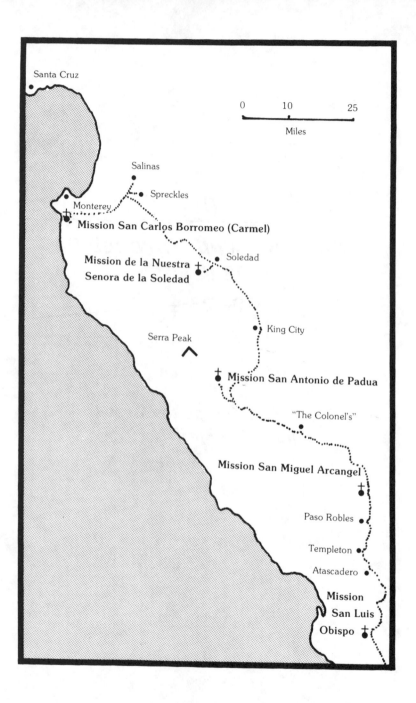

Santa Cruz

Salinas

Spreckles

Monterey

Mission San Carlos Borromeo (Carmel)

Mission de la Nuestra Soledad
Senora de la Soledad

Serra Peak

King City

Mission San Antonio de Padua

"The Colonel's"

Mission San Miguel Arcangel

Paso Robles

Templeton

Atascadero

**Mission
San Luis
Obispo**

0   10   25

Miles

Saturday, March 24: Feast of the Annunciation

"I don't envy you that grade," the pastor quipped, pressing a tightly-folded ten dollar bill into my palm. He had spent the previous evening guiding me on a tour of the sights of San Luis Obispo. Our parting was marked with affection and regret.

"That grade," crossing the Santa Lucia Mountains at the Cuesta Pass, rose more than fourteen hundred feet in less than five miles. It began just north of the city. With shin splints it would have been impossible, but Mary's prayers had worked. Apart from a little stiffness, my legs were fine. I took a leisurely pace, enjoyed the sun, and was over the crest by noon.

Just beyond the sleepy village of Santa Margarita, a small car pulled up from behind and stopped next to me. For a second I thought I was hallucinating. Then my mouth dropped open. It was Kevin and Mark, two of my neighbors from Berkeley.

"What on earth are *you* doing here?" I blurted.

"We came to take you out to lunch."

I became like an excited puppy, hugging them and repeating inanely, "I don't believe you're really here."

On vacation from grad school, they were making their way to San Diego for a week of camping. When they hit San Luis Obispo, they had looked at their map and guessed that I would be nearby. "You just missed him," they were

133

told at the mission. "Drive up the grade and through Santa Margarita and you should catch him." And they did.

We drove ahead to Atascadero and filled ourselves with Mexican food, beer, and stories about the past three weeks. It seemed like much longer since we had last seen each other. Being together uncovered the loneliness I had been ignoring, but I was too energized and ebullient to let it get me down.

Shortly before three Mark and Kevin continued south. I headed for a dot on the map called Templeton, six miles north.

Templeton was just a couple of farm houses. The first one on the left looked inviting. A short man in his fifties was tilling the land behind the house with a gas-powered hand plow. His shepherd dog saw me and bounded forward, barking menacingly. Since I stood my ground and showed no fear, the dog calmed down and started sniffing me curiously. The man looked up, stopped his plow, and walked toward me. By this time I had made friends with the dog.

The farmer agreed to let me stay the night. "I have no room in the house, though. You'll have to stay in the barn. There's a pile of hay out there. You can climb up and make yourself a bed."

I thanked him and asked if he had a heavy blanket or something I could cover myself with. He stepped to the garage and handed me a thick, dark-green, quilted horse blanket.

My next trick was to get in. The barn doors were padlocked. I did not want to make a nuisance of myself, so I climbed up and let myself in through the loading bay.

Then I saw the hay. I had imagined a big pile of loose hay that I could snuggle into for comfort and warmth. But we are no longer living in the age of Tom Sawyer. When the farmer had said "pile," he had meant "bales," as in "hard and prickly." No snuggling tonight! The bales were piled eight to twelve feet high in different places, and I had no intention of sleeping that far from the ground. If I fell off, I would see Berkeley sooner than I wanted to. So I hefted four of them down with a pitchfork and shoved them together to make a bed against the base of the main stack.

Then I thought of food. I had not been hungry when I was talking with the farmer, nor was I yet. But it was clear that there would be no supper that evening, nor breakfast in the morning. Suddenly I perceived the hand of the Lord. I had eaten a heavy Mexican meal between two and three, so I did not really need supper. And rather than being broke, I had the pastor's ten-dollar bill in my pocket. I could buy breakfast in the next town, Paso Robles. In addition, I had a couple of tangerines and a sandwich in my pack for the road between there and San Miguel. I shook my head in wonder. It was all too neat to be mere coincidence.

Darkness closed in at about seven. There was nothing to do but try to sleep. The barn was already getting chilly, and I was becoming aware of what I had gotten myself into. "Beggars can't be choosers," I recited, but that did not make me warm. I rolled up inside the horse blanket fully clothed, with my boots on and my watchcap down over my ears, eyes, and nose. Bunching into the fetal position, I pulled the blanket over my head for added warmth. And then I choked. Gasping for fresh air, I wrenched the blanket away from my face. It really was a horse blanket, and the odor of horse was so thick and foul that I could not breathe with it anywhere near my nose. This was going to be a longer night than I had foreseen.

A couple of horses came to a manger attached to the outside of the barn and started chomping. Far into the night I heard the gentle hollow mulching in their mouths. That was punctuated a couple of times by the rattling of the Southern Pacific just across the river. Why couldn't I have picked a barn farther from the tracks?

All night long I lay huddled on the prickly bales trying to stay warm and trying to keep my shoulders, back, and legs from cramping. I dozed at times, but every half hour I raised the watchcap from my nose and eyes to look for the half-light of dawn. Each time I would get a smack of frigid air. But morning would not come. The night was so cold that I kept trying to figure out a way of using the blanket for my head without dying of asphyxiation. I reminded myself several times that if a barn had been good enough for Jesus, it should be good enough for me. Even that did not keep me warm.

A cock crowed in the distance. Morning? No. Still dark. I waited and shivered through the longest night I could remember. After what seemed like about forty-eight hours, I heard the faint chirping of birds. Again I peered out, but this time I saw dim gray light. Enough light to walk. I was on my feet immediately.

Sunday, March 25.

Desiring to be away from there as fast as possible, I folded the blanket, packed my things, and was over the barn doors in record time.

Morning was still cold and eerily quiet. Along the eight miles of country road from Templeton to Paso Robles I saw one pedestrian, two cars, and three horses. The last were the most interesting. Sauntering majestically to the edge of the road, they watched with placid interest as I passed. Their bearing reminded me of the Christ-figure in the play *Equus*.[8] They seemed to say, "Well, if you insist on entering our world, we suppose we can't stop you. Know, however, that you are an inferior breed."

The only place open for breakfast was The Paso Robles Inn, two or three cuts above my current level of society. The menus were padded leather. I felt as out of place as I looked. The hostess and waitress were personable and gracious, which put me at ease. The other diners, most of them in their Sunday best, seemed not to notice me. I ordered a breakfast that bordered on gluttony.

Mission San Miguel lay ten miles ahead, including a two-mile backtrack after crossing the river. Notable features of the walk were heat, boredom, and fatigue. My body carried the effects of a sleepless night, which were aggravated by a strong sun and a deserted road. I walked in a daze, reality a quarter-step away. In this state I intuited that a major obstacle during the final weeks could be ennui. Might I have become so languorous as to lack the will to go on? Almost as if tempting the Lord, I thought, "Things have gone pretty well. Almost too well."

Instantly the voice within was stirred: "Don't worry. I can still test you. Are you willing to meet adversities that will make the past look tame? I can try you to the core, if you want me to."

The romantic in me wanted to say, "Yes, Lord." The realist wanted to run. Between them I came up with a sober and faltering, "Whatever you choose, Lord. Only let me know that I'm doing your will."

I arrived at Mission San Miguel Arcangel at 2:00 P.M. It stood at the south end of one of the sleepiest hang-dog towns I had ever seen. Years ago the freeways had diverted traffic away, so San Miguel stood still. The only business open on Sunday was the saloon, and even that was quiet.

I told the girl at the Mission gift shop that I was a Jesuit priest and asked if I could speak with the pastor. She rang him on an in-house phone.

"Fr. Hilary, would you come up front, please." Hanging up she said to me, "He'll be right out."

"Just like that?" I asked. "Didn't he ask why you wanted him to come?"

"No, he just comes," she replied matter-of-factly.

That was my introduction to a man for whom I was to develop a deep affection before the end of the day. Fr. Hilary, O.F.M. appeared in black pants and a light gray bus-boy's jacket. An older man with glasses and snow white hair, he stood slightly taller than myself. He spoke softly and haltingly, as if having suffered a slight stroke. He reacted to my appearance and story with perfect equanimity and led me straight to a guest room. When I asked if there were a parish Mass at which I could concelebrate, he invited me to preside at the 4:00 P.M. children's service and tell them about my journey.

During the homily I walked up and down the center aisle. "What is a pilgrim?" I asked the children. Silent stares. Either they did not know or they were embarrassed. I decided to carry the ball myself. "A pilgrim is someone who is on the road with Jesus. He walks with Jesus and lets Jesus take care of everything he needs. He talks with Jesus as he walks along the road. You are all pilgrims, too. We are all on the road of life, and Jesus walks next to us all the time. The important thing is to turn to him and trust him in everything."

The children were marvelous. After Mass a handful of them, all black-haired and dark-eyed Mexicans, surrounded Father Hilary, chattering and hugging him. The glint in his eyes showed that the feeling was mutual. They played so comfortably in the church. The Lord's house was theirs. Before long, I, too, was receiving my share of hugs.

Back in the friary the pastor and I heated leftovers for dinner. We ate at a little table in the kitchen. During the meal I mentioned my affinity for St. Francis and my devotion to the crucifix of San Damiano. Fr. Hilary was on his feet. He led me into the next room, the community refectory. On the far wall hung a life-size reproduction of the crucifix. To my own surprise and Fr. Hilary's I spontaneously dropped to my knees.

When we had finished eating and cleaning up, I asked if I could use a phone to call Berkeley. Fr. Hilary said, "Follow me." We wended our way through the dark walkways surrounding the courtyard. I thought, "This is awfully far to go for a phone." When the lights blinked on, we stood in the gift shop. My quiet companion surveyed the room, glancing cryptically in all directions until he found what he wanted. Picking up a pocket-sized replica of the San Damiano cross, he handed it to me. Before I could thank him, he had darted to the opposite wall and was taking down a large version of the same crucifix. It stood almost twenty inches high and was framed in gold leaf. Pointing to a note pad on the counter, the Franciscan said, "Write your name and address here. I'm going to mail this to you."

I hesitated. "I can't accept that, Father. You're very kind, but it's too big a gift."

"No, it's not," he softly assured me. "Write your address."

I obeyed, speechless and on the verge of tears. Three weeks later, when I arrived home, the cross was on my bed. That was not all, though. A thick envelope awaited me, containing fourteen letters thanking me for the Mass and homily. They had been written by the children.

Monday, March 26.

I started the day restless and apprehensive. A gray sky threatened rain. The next mission, San Antonio, lay two days ahead, with nothing in the middle but wilderness and an occasional mobile home. Two specks of village appeared on the map, one too near to stop for the night, the other too far. In addition there was no evidence of a decent route. The walkable road seemed discouragingly roundabout. More direct were a freeway, a train track, and the dried bed of the Salinas River. I opted for the last. Finally, I was concerned about my feet. The middle toes were going numb. My boots were loose enough and there was no discoloration, so the problem was not circulatory. I concluded that the nerve endings were succumbing to the gentle but incessant blows of walking.

At breakfast the Franciscans cautioned me against the riverbed's unpredictability. In some spots it could be quicksand; in others it could be flooded. They favored the tracks. Trains were rare and easily heard in the distance. When I asked if walking the railroad were allowed, one brother replied, "Well, it's not against the moral law, just the legal law." He would have made a good Jesuit.

Old Brother Cyril thought about my route and the impending rain. "I have some good friends who live half way to San Antonio. They'd love to put you up. Want me to call them?"

I turned him down, saying that I really should take my own chances with begging. He dropped it for about two minutes.

"It's mighty barren out there, and you'll probably be in rain. Why don't you let me call them? They'd be sorry if they found out you'd gone by." Again I held off.

The third time he brought it up I gave in, thinking, "Maybe this is the Lord's way of providing." Brother Cyril hopped up and grabbed a nearby phone. A minute later I was speaking with Russell and Helen. They lived right on my route, just midway between the two missions, and they sounded genuinely eager to give me hospitality. I estimated my arrival time, and they told me how to identify their home. As I turned away from the phone, Brother Cyril read relief on my face and broke out in a satisfied and childlike grin.

Three miles out a soft, steady rain began to fall. At about the same time a country road appeared alongside the tracks. Why it was not on my map and why the Franciscans had failed to mention it is still a mystery to me. Since it made walking safer, easier, and legal, I switched.

A few miles short of Bradley I had to cross the river at a point where the flow was wide and the bridges long. If the county road had not been there, I would have been forced to use the railway trestle fifty yards to my right. That struck me as risky, though I had not seen a train all morning. Ironically I was midway across when a fast-moving freight train roared over the trestle. Picturing myself jumping into the river or dangling by my pack straps from the end of a crossbeam, I thanked the Lord profusely for the road.

The rain shrank my world as I glided tranquilly through rolling hay country in my plastic cocoon. For eight or ten miles the valley narrowed, until I had low hills immediately on both sides. At about the time that weariness and drizzle were beginning to get the best of me, I looked up and recognized my destination. Half a mile directly ahead, with an excellent command of the valley, a double-wide mobile home perched high above the road. Approaching it on foot reminded me of the homecoming of the Prodigal Son. "While he was still a long way off, his father caught sight of him and was deeply moved. He ran out to meet him, threw his arms around his neck, and kissed him" (Lk 15:20). My hosts did not go that far, but they did see me in the distance and watched from the porch as I neared their gate and wound up the driveway.

Russell and Helen were retired, having raised five children. They lived alone and cultivated intimacy with the earth, the animals, and the wildflowers. Dinner was a batch of fresh trout that Russell had caught. Slender and serious-looking, he talked in a clipped, Yankee style. Actually his roots were in Missouri. I think his little white goatee had something to do with his nickname, "The Colonel." He was not a Catholic, though he faithfully attended Mass with his wife, who was a simple and devout communicant.

Hospitality was in both Helen's and Russell's blood, probably from decades of practice. Helen overcame her impulse to treat me with vigilant deference, yielding to her stronger inclination toward maternal affection and solicitude. The Colonel made me feel at home by opening up to me his interest in nature and hunting. Both Russell and Helen suppressed, for the most part, any show of being honored at my presence, though it crept out occasionally. They intuited correctly that I just wanted to be one of them.

Tuesday, March 27.

Mission San Antonio de Padua, my next stop, stood nineteen miles away in Hunter Liggett Military Reservation, beyond the villages of Lockwood and Jolon. The whole route would be through sparsely populated woodlands and grazing country.

Morning sunshine was only a teaser. Soon the sky darkened and large drops danced off the macadam. Out came the poncho and garbage bags. I had to hold the poncho closed at my throat because the thin plastic had torn down several inches.

The weather dulled my spirits. I ceased to be interested in being where I was. I just wanted to get out of the gloom and wetness and arrive at the mission. My pack seemed very heavy. Prayer came hard. I got angry at the storm, then at God for sending it. Wind rushed against me, stirring up my rage. Remembering the inner voice of two days earlier, I tried to accept the weather as one of those adversities that were for my own good. "Lord, make me more simple and humble. Give me simplicity like Peter's. Or like your own."

He answered, "I will purify you in suffering. I will teach you the meaning of love. I will teach you how to really love."

Then the desert experience of boredom set in. There was not even traffic to break the monotony. My spirits slipped into neutral, protecting themselves against the outside world. I tramped along in an automatic marching step. No thoughts; just rhythmic body movement. Mesmerized. I could not pray. I just plodded on, wishing I were already at San Antonio and offering my boredom to God. Some gift!

I felt pressured to get to the mission, not relaxed and free as I thought I should be. I wondered if I were still making pilgrimage a "job." Sometimes I felt as if I were just rushing from mission to mission to get it done and be able to say I had done it. I had been around that mulberry bush several times already. "Maybe I should slow down," I thought. Then I objected, "How can I do that? There's nowhere to stop in this wilderness. So what do I do?"

The answer was not long in coming: "Just be. Concentrate on the present moment. Try to be present with the Lord, so that walking becomes secondary, like background music to the real pilgrimage inside."

Peace returned.

Some time after midday a green sedan came from behind and stopped next to me. Russell, grinning ever so slightly, greeted me with, "I know you can't take a ride; but you can stop and have a cup of hot soup, can't you? Even Jesus had help carrying his cross." I sat in the car and drank two cups of chicken noodle soup and listened to more lore about the territory. As Russell talked, I thought, "What kind of man drives ten miles one way to bring a thermos of hot soup to an almost-stranger?"

On parting I made a pact with the Colonel: "Say a prayer for me, Russell, and I'll say one for you."

"I surely will," the clipped Yankee voice bounced back. "That's the best thing any man can do for another."

Broad, flat cattle ranges stretched far away to the hills on both sides. The day had gradually improved, and ahead of me was bright sunshine, broken only by white, fluffy clouds. A friendly breeze was drying my poncho. The black storm clouds were all behind me to the left. Then suddenly the wind changed. I looked over my left shoulder in time to see an angry curtain of cloud and rain racing toward me. Within two minutes I was being drenched.

That seemed like a lousy trick. I had paid my dues for the day. Now I was wet again. And mad. The Father gently cut in. He reminded me that my purification was his concern and that my anger itself testified to my need for more. What he provided would always be what was best for me. Could I rejoice in what came from his hand, even if it felt unpleasant?

Again peace returned.

The last six miles were better. No more rain. The sky even seemed to be clearing. Four miles along, my poncho was almost dry. I judged that I had seen the end of precipitation for that day. Sitting on the ground I took off the poncho and garbage bags, not wanting to arrive at the mission looking like a refugee from a plastics factory. The bags had served their purpose more by keeping my legs warm than dry. My jeans were damp, but the wrappings had contained my body heat.

Dead ahead in the distance a long red-tiled roof peeked timidly over a slight rise in the road. Immediately behind it towered the Santa Lucia Range, with foothills reaching past me on both sides. Serra Peak, twelve miles directly beyond, butted against the low, smoky cloud ceiling. As I drew near, Mission San Antonio de Padua slowly rose above the false horizon created by the bulge in the valley floor and, when fully visible, lay nestled in the embrace of the mountains. The approach was thrilling. The mission church dominated the right end, while the arcade flowed to the left. The grounds were kept in their pristine state with high, wild grass and weeds, as at La Purisima. Of all the missions, none can compare with San Antonio for authentic, unspoiled, and outstandingly beautiful surroundings.

San Antonio was only the third mission Fr. Serra founded. During July 1771, after establishing San Diego and San Carlos Borromeo, the old Franciscan wandered into this valley with two companions. They hoisted a large bronze bell from a mule-pack and hung it on a low tree branch. After a period of silent prayer, Father Serra filled the valley and the mountains with roundly crashing bell-tones and with his own cries: "Oh, you Gentiles! Come! Come to the holy church! Come to receive the faith of Jesus Christ!" Thus was founded the mission honoring St. Anthony of Padua. He probably would have smiled at such a spirited beginning.

The mission was a quiet place maintained by only two Franciscans, Brother Timothy and Father Joe, who led almost eremitical lives. San Antonio is, after all, pretty far off the beaten path, like San Miguel. When I commented about the isolation, Brother Timothy jested drily, pointing toward the floor, "Don't worry. The way things are expanding, some day San Francisco and Los Angeles will meet right here."

Brother Timothy was a quiet man in his thirties, slender, moderately tall, with thinning sandy hair. Father Joe was just the opposite: short, stocky, and in his fifties. He had graying hair, wore rimless glasses, and was a talker. Both men dressed informally, as befitted the atmosphere of the house.

Supper was simple. Father Joe heated three home-made frozen dinners prepared by a friend in Oakland. She supplied them regularly.

Dark clouds gathered while we ate, and before dessert the rain was again falling hard.

While soaking in a hot bath I reflected that I seemed to be getting accustomed to having no home or bed of my own. I no longer thought much about the verse, "The Son of Man has nowhere to lay his head." Was I getting dulled to begging or being homeless? Was I taking God's gifts for granted? More likely I was developing necessary defenses, growing nonchalant as a way of coping with my situation. The frequency of baths seemed part of the same pattern. At home I usually took showers. Now the regular immersion in hot water was something I almost depended on, like a return to the womb or the protection of a maternal embrace. It had not been a conscious decision, but an instinctive adaptation of an organism to its environment: a homeless body in motion seeking primal stasis.

Wednesday, March 28.

Leaving Mission San Antonio was not easy. Its pristine beauty and rustic setting made me stop several times to look back. Forcing myself to move ahead, I turned my attention toward King City, twenty miles away, down in the Salinas Valley. High dark clouds were rolling in menacingly. I walked with my poncho in my hand.

Soon I found myself dwarfed in a maze of high hills that seemed to have popped up suddenly and with no apparent order. They were roughly cone-shaped and free-standing, close enough together to cause the road to weave around their bases on its way north. Vast exposed faces of layered, sedimentary rock rose up in massive folds and inclines. I was awed at hundreds of millions of tons of pre-historic sea-floor that had been thrust up and tilted at angles of fifty and sixty degrees. My college geology led me to suspect that I was on the edge of one continental plate which had been lifted for hundreds of millions of years by the edge of another. The time and forces involved in such a process made my lifespan seem gnatlike and fleeting. I began to feel microscopic and unimportant in the presence of the God who could do all this.

As I rounded a bend my musings were interrupted by a pack of five bulls grazing just off the left side of the road. There was no fence. I walked along the far shoulder without changing pace. One of the bulls, a black one, stared at me and snorted, causing the others to notice me. When I was nearly even with them, the one who had snorted ran ahead twenty yards, stopped, and continued to gawk. I clunked the butt of my stick loudly on the pavement in rhythm with my steps. Seeing me proceed, the lone bull

146

ran farther ahead, stopped, and eyed me still. My clunking continued. I tried to show no fear, keeping an even moderate gait. Having four bulls behind me and one ahead did not do much for my peace of soul. When I was almost parallel to the front bull, he started running again, this time back to the pack. Somewhat relieved but still fearful, I glanced back occasionally to see the five of them gaping at me until I was almost out of sight around the next bend. At the last minute, they went back to grazing. Robert Frost was right: "Good fences make good neighbors."

The sky darkened and a cold wind blew in from the north. Not long after I reached the country road and turned north toward King City, a light rain started. I put on my poncho and climbed gradually through twisting canyons to the crest of the Jolon Grade. Before me spread an exhilarating vista of the Salinas Valley, with mountains beyond. I descended the long grade and found the valley warmer, protected from the wind. I was actually in a foothill canyon running out from the southwest wall of the main valley.

I passed the time by meditating on my relationships with the people I had met thus far, people whose lives I had entered for a few hours or even a few minutes. It occurred to me that after I left them, the ones who remembered me would know precious little about me. They were ignorant of my family history or faith development, my likes and dislikes, my desires and fears. All I was to them was what they had seen and heard: a walking pilgrim without money, dependent on God and people. I would be less a person to them than a symbol. From their comments I gathered that I symbolized different things to different people, according to their own history and needs. To some I was the personification of perseverance. A brother at San Miguel had called me a "tough hombre." For others I symbolized fidelity to a call, devotion, holiness, union with God, or penitence. Many saw me as a man who had broken free of the bonds of contemporary capitalism. A few just

147

thought I was a fool or a hopeless romantic, but even they—some of them—envied me.

I could accept being a symbol. The pilgrimage was giving me a transparency. People could see through Dick Roos to the Gospel. If they did not know or remember *me,* that was all right. They would remember the pilgrimage and might ponder what it said to them about themselves. Some might hear it for the first time long after I had ambled away. Others might not hear it at all. That was a discipline for me, going against my need to see results and be a success. I could accept that, too.

What bothered me was how much I was enjoying people's reactions to the oddity of my journey, which eclipsed my ordinariness as a person. My need to be special and admired, a manifestation of inner insecurity, was being fed. Seeing myself currying people's interest and adulation, and knowing myself to be so much smaller and less integrated than the person they were applauding, I began to chastise myself mentally. I blamed myself for a kind of prophetic dishonesty. Even that was an inflation of reality. Ironically, under the guise of a poor pilgrim I was hiding my real poverty—a poverty of ego that I was as terrified to reveal to myself as to others. Under that particular light the whole pilgrimage was a deception which I guiltily resented. Yet under other lights it was truth, and I knew that, too. The challenge was to learn to live with both simultaneously, while trying to bring appearance and reality into congruence.

When I reached King City, begging for lodging proved to be an adventure. People wanted to help me—by directing me to someone else. At the first two houses I received a simple refusal and nobody home.

Third house: an old lady. "I can't take you in, but try that house across the street. He's a minister and might help you."

I went where she had directed. A pleasant woman answered the door, listened to my request, and called her husband. He asked, "What group are you with?"

"I'm a Catholic."

"Are you a born-again Christian?"

"Yes, sir."

"Well, I'm a Baptist and I think the Catholics ought to patronize you. There's a Catholic church two blocks over. Just take a left at the corner up there."

"Thank you sir."

Next house: a woman around forty, seemingly well-intentioned and wanting to help. "There's a Dr. So-and-so at Such-and-such church. He's the minister there. He has a set-up to take care of transients in your situation. Just go down two blocks, take a right, and you'll come to the church."

"Thank you, ma'am."

By the time the woman had given me instructions, the Baptist gentleman had come out of his house and was on the sidewalk waiting for me.

"Are you hungry?"

"No, sir. Not yet. I will be in a couple of hours, though."

"Oh." He seemed disappointed. "If you were hungry I'd feed you."

"That's very kind of you, sir. But my problem is that if I went in to eat now, it would be dark when I came out, and it's impossible to get lodging in the dark. But thank you, anyway."

Sixth house: a young Mexican couple with small children. The husband worked nights. He apparently wanted to help me but was afraid to leave me alone with his wife and children. "Why don't you try next door? If you can't get a place, come back here and we'll see what we can do." He sounded sincere.

Seventh house: a strapping, middle-aged, cheerful gentleman who answered the door with a smile and an aggressive "Hi!" The smile faded as my story unfolded. When I finished, he jumped right in: "You want to go to the police. They have a hacienda for people passing through town."

"Thank you, sir."

"Do you know where the police department is?"

"No, sir."

"Do you want to know?"

"No, sir. You see, I've met such good people and made such fine friends staying at homes along the way, I'd rather not turn to institutions at this point."

"Oh, this isn't an institution. It's a very nice setup that the police department runs."

"I understand, sir. And I thank you. But I'm a Catholic, and if I can't get anyone to take me in, I'll go to the Catholic rectory."

"O.K."

Next house: an old lady. "No, I live here with my small son and we don't have any room. Do you want to go to the Pentecostal church?"

With all this advice and no place to stay, I was ready to give up. In fact I did give up. Rounding the corner to the left, I headed toward the Catholic church. But I was unhappy. I really wanted to get lodging from ordinary citizens. Part of me wanted to succeed as a beggar, too. While these thoughts rolled around in my head, I came upon a white house with shrubbery on the corner of a side street. It looked so homey and inviting that I stepped over for a closer look. A vaguely Italian-looking name hung on a black metal plate out front. I remembered the words of Tony Cantelmi, one of the tertians from my community in Berkeley: "If you're ever stuck, go to an Italian home. They'll always take you in." I hoped it was true, and I hoped this name was Italian. A woman in her sixties answered the door. She had kind eyes. Having listened to

150

my story, she looked at her husband for support and invited me in.

Still dripping wet, I was afraid of harming the carpet. Before I had stepped fully inside, the woman had taken my poncho and boots to a back room and had given me a pair of crocheted slippers. The three of us sat in the kitchen and talked while the woman cooked dinner.

Helen and Elvin were Episcopalians, both retired school teachers, and the parents of three grown children: a daughter, 40, and two sons, 36 and 32. Elvin was a retired major in the army. Their name was not Italian. They possessed a wisdom and gentleness that convinced me they had learned a great deal about life through suffering and love. Their voices were peaceful and their outlook was calmly cheerful.

Helen had to go out to a birthday party for one of her girlfriends, so with a little coaxing I got her to let me do the dishes. Elvin watched TV and fell asleep in front of it. I took a bath and read and wrote in my journal. The guestroom was neat and comfortable, with a Bible on the night table and Sallman's head of Christ attached to the corner of the bureau mirror.

The numbness in my toes was concerning me more, though color and circulation seemed normal. I tried to convince myself it was just temporary deadening of the nerves, similar to a case of frostbite I had experienced in high school when my ski boots had been too tight. If it were that, it would pass after a few weeks back home. If it were something more serious, I would watch for more critical symptoms. Meanwhile I would try to put it into the hands of the Lord.

Thursday, March 29.

The weather seemed to be improving. I had decided that three rainy days in a row were enough, and I was hoping the Lord had come to the same conclusion.

During breakfast I asked Helen if she had told her girl-friends about her unexpected guest.

"Yes, I did."

"What did they say?"

She responded as I had anticipated, almost verbatim: "They said, 'Weren't you afraid?'"

"And how did you answer?" I pressed.

Helen stopped her work at the counter. She looked at me, then stared off into space. "I told them, 'No. For some reason I wasn't. Normally I would be, but not this time.'"

Our conversation turned to the subject of God's providence and I told some stories of how the Lord had taken care of me. Then Elvin, who was usually silent, his diction apparently hampered from a mild stroke, began to speak. "I was in a plane crash on Lake Superior. A half mile off shore in a hundred and eight feet of water. The water temperature was thirty-nine degrees. I swam and swam until I couldn't swim any more. I gave up and thought it was the end. Then I looked up . . . and there was a boat right in front of me." His voice cracked a little and he put a hand over his eyes.

From King City, the Salinas River Valley runs directly northwest fifty-five miles to Monterey Bay. It averages eight miles across, widening out at the coast. The river meanders lazily back and forth across its floor, emptying into the bay near Castroville. Freeway 101 streaks directly up the middle. Rich with vegetables, this land spelled salvation during the Depression for the "Okies" from the midwest dustbowl, like Steinbeck's Joad family.[9] Today the Joads come from Mexico.

The valley is a perfect wind tunnel. All day every day the northwest wind sweeps down from Monterey Bay, as reliable as the wind on the Dakota prairies. With nothing to stop it, and with parallel ranges of mountains to guide it, it brings coolness and moisture from the sea. It is a blessing, but also a curse. Few things in the world can wear away human souls as effectively as relentless, whistling wind.

The sky was partly cloudy. A cool wind pushed against me. I had low hills on my right and flat farmland on my left, across which rose the Santa Lucia Range of the Los Padres Mountains that dropped down to the Pacific on their western side. Snow-capped Serra Peak gleamed in the sunlight that shot between the clouds.

Sitting by the side of the road about midday, I looked south along the straight, desolate ribbon as far as I could see, then turned my gaze north. There was nothing. Just road, hills, valley, and wind. No houses. No traffic. A question framed itself in my mind: "What in heaven's name am I doing out here in the middle of nowhere without money or provisions?" As soon as it was formulated, I blocked myself from answering it. Instead I told myself, somewhat convincingly, that the world was now my home and that I was at home wherever Jesus was. It was a defense, but it enabled me to get up and walk on in peace.

Later I caught myself trying to figure out how to cope with Soledad Mission. According to my maps, the mission site was four or five miles beyond the town of Soledad, but to the southwest. Being an uninhabited ruin with a small replica of the original chapel, the mission could offer no lodging. I would ask to stay in town at the parish that was descended from the mission, as at Lompoc. The trick was to get there with a minimum time loss and as few extra steps as possible. If I went to the mission and doubled back to the rectory, the day's walk would add up to thirty miles. If I stopped at the parish I would have to swing around to the mission in the morning and celebrate Mass there, then go on to Spreckels, a total of thirty miles tomorrow, not counting the time consumed by the mission visit. I had all but decided to skip the rectory and go directly to the mission and seek lodging nearby, avoiding the five-mile return to town. "No, that's wrong. Don't bypass the pastor of a mission," I thought. So I was hung up. A voice within me was awakened: "Put yourself into my hands. Don't try to be smart. Don't try to second-guess me. I've taken care of you in the past, and I'll do it now. Trust me. Just go to the rectory and leave the rest to me." I decided to obey the voice, and my peace returned.

Turning slightly left toward the town of Soledad, Route 146 took me into the full force of the wind with no hills to protect me. Walking became a battle. I leaned into the wall of rushing air. That lasted about an hour and a half.

Cold and frazzled, I rang the rectory bell just shy of four o'clock. The pastor himself answered. Gray-haired and bespectacled, he was very Irish, not too tall, and wore a many-buttoned black cassock. He seemed somewhat inconvenienced by my arrival, since he was about to step out for Lenten confessions. I asked if I could stay the night. Yes, I could. How far was it to the mission and would I have time to celebrate Mass there before dinner this evening? Yes, there would be time. It was only two and a half miles. Maybe three. I was surprised and pleased. My maps had erred. The priest gave me directions and assured me I could get into the chapel. There was a live-in caretaker. I had better take things for Mass, though. There was nothing at the mission.

Grabbing my little wine bottle, hosts, purificator, and missalette, I left my pack and stick at the rectory and bounded out. Leaving the pack and stick behind was partly to be free of them, but partly to win the pastor's trust and to establish squatter's rights at the rectory.

Reaching the edge of town I was again in direct opposition to the wind. I bucked it with all my might. Two miles out I met a sign: "Soledad Mission 3 Miles." My maps had not erred. It really *was* five miles. The priest had been mistaken. I began to see how badly things were going. My host was not too happy about my arrival; I would have to do thirty miles today; the sun would be down soon and I would have to walk back to town in the dark and be late for supper, adding to the pastor's displeasure with me; and the wind was blowing every holy sentiment out of my head and heart. Had I been wrong when I thought I was hearing the Lord make that speech about not planning ahead?

I continued to fight the wind. It cut through my windbreaker and sweater, chilling me to the bone. I was miserable and angry. All I could see were miles of fields and a couple of farm houses. "Where's the damn mission? Why have you done this to me, God?"

"Trust me," came the voice, calmly.

No sooner had it spoken than an open gate appeared on the left side of the road just beyond the nearest farmhouse. Shrubbery decorated it on both sides, and the ruins of Soledad Mission came into view from behind the house. Then the voice said, "The caretaker will drive you home." My trust returned and I felt ashamed of my anger. Like the mission, I had been a victim of the wind.

Mission de la Nuestra Senora de la Soledad (The Mission of Our Lady of Solitude) had been well named. It was, and still is, the loneliest mission of all. It stood as the thirteenth in the chain, both by location and by order of founding. Whether one is superstitious or not, its fortyfour year history of active service marked Soledad as the least successful and the most battered of all the missions. The unfriendly climate, with its cold, damp, and windy winters, kept the padres and the natives ill and rheumatic much of the time. The isolated region yielded few Indian converts. Without modern techniques, agriculture was nowhere near as successful as it is today. Soledad was abandoned in 1835. Instead of simply falling into disrepair and ruin, the mission was literally blown away. All that is left today are a few stubs of adobe walls, eroded and swept clean. Nearby stands a small chapel in memory of the Franciscans who labored there.

The chapel was locked down tight when I arrived, but the caretaker's son Randy let me in and agreed to drive me back to the rectory after Mass. Randy and his parents lived in a mobile home behind the mission. It struck me as appropriate that I should celebrate the Eucharist at Soledad completely alone and with an impromptu Mass kit. Loneliness still broods over the ruins.

Randy's father brought me back to town. When I arrived, the pastor was more cordial. Apparently his earlier aloofness had been caused by his rush to get to confessions. The priest lived alone and cooked for himself, so the two of us got to know each other in the kitchen while he broiled a couple of steaks, along with fresh carrots and asparagus from the valley. We got into a long conversation about the pastor's native County Mayo. After the meal we adjourned to the living room, where we continued until almost 10:00 P.M. We spoke of renewal in the Church and of theological updating of the clergy. My host proved to be a simple and good-hearted priest on whom much of Vatican II was lost. Not that he opposed changes in the Church. Rather he did not see how they were of much use to him all alone out there in Soledad with his flock of laborers. "The change to English was good, mind you. But as for the rest of it, the Mass is the Mass and confession is confession. Always has been. It's what the people are comfortable with." I had to work at seeing beyond my disagreement with him in order not to miss the more basic goodness of the man who had opened his home to me.

Friday, March 30.

My sleep had been shallow. Short of Spreckels was nothing but open fields, and I had been worried about covering the twenty-five miles against the mindless wind. Less than fifteen minutes out it was so fierce I had to duck behind an overpass to get out of the blast and put on more clothing. Over my shirt and sweater I added two more shirts and a windbreaker, theorizing that the sweater would insulate me by trapping warm air under the three outer layers. My watchcap was down over my ears.

At forty miles per hour the wind bit through everything, chilling me still. My loose jacket flapped like a rapidly snapping flag. I leaned stubbornly into the flow and pushed myself forward with my staff. Rushing air roared past my ears, robbing me of all peace and concentration. Its constant impersonal opposition made me want to scream aloud, "Enough! Stop!" I brandished my staff at the sky like a frustrated old man chasing vandals. It did a lot of good. "Just one day," I told myself. "It's only for one day." In a second I would have traded that wind for a downpour.

I tramped against the wind for the next eight hours. When I was able to pray, it consisted of asking that some good come from this. I wanted my spirit to be purified and simplified. It was as if I believed that somehow the wind could blow away my complexity and the divisions within my heart. The kind of love I was praying to be able to generate was still naive and idealized. But I noticed an encouraging change in my motivation. My prayer was no longer coming out of mere intellectual conviction. Instead I was praying for something I really wanted for myself. I was praying honestly. And the prayer was not that I conquer the wind, but that it conquer me. Unlike the spiritual machismo that had inflated my earlier prayer and dictated a scheduled program of interior advancement, this new prayer was genuinely that I be emptied and disposed for whatever the Lord willed. I felt myself beginning to be freed of my own expectations of myself. But I still had a long way to go.

The town of Spreckels, I discovered, lay across the river, accessible only by a five-mile detour. The sun was getting low, so I decided to try for hospitality along the road. I stopped at the first house I came to. A young woman with a small boy listened kindly but told me it was her parents' house and they were not home. She offered to drive me to Spreckels. The wind had blown away enough of my pride for me to accept. At that point the path of least resistance looked mighty fine. The pastor in town had no room for me in his small cottage, so he urged me to let him take me to Salinas, five miles in the wrong direction. That would make the next day's walk longer. Not having the energy to seek elsewhere, I acquiesced.

The priest delivered me to the steps of Sacred Heart Rectory. My finger was an inch from the bell when the door opened. Startled, I looked up into the smiling eyes of a ruddy-faced Irish associate pastor in his early forties. He was happy to give me a room.

Upstairs, as I dropped my pack on the bed, a booming voice barreled down the hall: "Hello! Hello!" Enter the whirlwind: a gaunt, white-haired monsignor who had been in Salinas for thirty years and who was vicar general for the Monterey diocese. He pumped my hand and bustled around making sure I had everything he thought I needed. He was followed close underfoot by two miniature dogs, a long-haired terrier named Colleen and a black poodle named Shortstop. Their first reactions to me were mock-heroic barks that sounded more like throaty chirps.

"Have you eaten?" asked the pastor, still in a hurry to provide for me.

"No, Monsignor."

"Come on! You must eat!" he bellowed in an oddly endearing fashion.

The priests had just finished their supper. On the dining room table was a leftover portion of fish, potatoes, and lima beans. It just needed to be heated up. The old priest rejected it and, after a brief rummage through the refrigerator, announced, "Come on! We're going out!" I tried to protest, but he would not hear it. "I have a conscience," he informed me. We went out.

I kept my eyes open for a hamburger stand or a short-order diner. That was not the pastor's definition of "going out." The norm was elegance. My blue jeans embarrassed me. So did the menu. I was told to order whatever I wanted. Having just eaten, the dear old monsignor nursed a glass of water and gave me an engaging autobiography. To please him I ate more than I really needed and told stories about my journey. I think we equally fascinated each other.

When we were leaving I noticed the name of the restaurant: "The Windfall." I was glad I had missed it on the way in. I would have lost my appetite.

Saturday, March 31.

For a variety of reasons I was anxious to reach Mission San Carlos Borromeo de Carmelo. I had been trekking in adverse conditions since San Luis Obispo and needed a day of rest, which I was envisioning for Carmel. This would mark the end of the most desolate and discouraging section of my route. Furthermore, Dennis Hamm was planning to drive down from my community in Berkeley to meet me for a visit. I really needed to see a familiar face. As if that were not enough, the mission at Carmel was my favorite. I had visited it a few months earlier and been charmed. Its natural setting near mountains and ocean was idyllic. Of all the missions I found its architecture most tasteful and most sensitively restored. Finally, it had been Fr. Serra's favorite, where he had chosen to retire, die, and be interred. This March 31 I had only one thing on my mind: Carmel.

My urgency imposed on the day a disoriented in-between-ness. Something had finished, but something else had not yet begun. It was like the waiting between death and resurrection. Today was an interior Holy Saturday, liturgically two weeks early. It felt eerie and disconnected, somber and vaguely hopeful.

I landed on the steps of the mission between three and four o'clock. The German housekeeper told me the pastor was hearing confessions. An associate showed me to a comfortable parlor and gave me a tall glass of ice cold water, leaving me then to wait.

The pastor was a slender man of medium height, in his fifties, bald, and wearing glasses. He had a shade of a brogue. At first the poor man seemed miffed by my presence and my request to stay for two nights. After a moment's hesitation he showed me to a guest room and determined that it was suitably prepared. I got the impression he still did not know what to make of me. He left me to rest.

Removing my boots I noted that numbness had spread across the whole front of my feet. There was no sensation forward of the arches, and I was getting worried. Remembering what I had done for the frostbite in high school, I soaked my feet in water as hot as I could endure it and decided to repeat the treatment as often as possible.

Concern for my feet raised anew the specter of not completing the pilgrimage, or, more precisely, of not reaching Sonoma. The pilgrimage would be complete wherever, whenever, and for whatever reason I chose or was forced to stop. The operative question was, "In my mind how much of the value of the experience rests on my walking the entire mission chain?" Another way of putting it was, "How much am I willing to risk for the distinction of having gone the whole way?" The trip had never been billed as an endurance test. I was the only person who was laying any expectations on Dick Roos. It was my need that I had to contend with, just as before—my need to measure my worth by external achievement. It discouraged me to admit it again. I prayed to be free, at least free enough to quit if that were the wiser and more honest choice.

At 5:45 the monsignor stuck his head into my room and asked playfully, "Do you indulge?" I joined the priests for a drink. Gunda, the woman who had answered the door, served a German dinner of pork, red cabbage, and potato dumplings. As we ate it became clear that the pastor had taken a shine to me. I traded my pilgrimage stories for his mission lore, which was mostly about Carmel. By the end of the meal he had invited me to preside at the eleven o'clock parish Mass the following morning. My Holy Saturday was flowing into an experience of Easter.

Sunday, April 1: Day of Rest

At 9:00 A.M. the church was empty between Masses, and the organ was playing softly. I walked slowly up the center aisle toward the high altar. Four months earlier I had prayed here and had promised to return. It had been the beginning of a love affair with Carmel Mission. Now I was keeping that promise, having walked five hundred and fifty miles to do it. I knelt at the sanctuary rail, my eyes fixed on the gray stone slab that marked the resting place of Fr. Serra. A bond had been forged between us. We had walked the same paths and breathed the same Spirit. In the last four weeks I had become, I felt, one of his progeny.

Outside I lingered in the spacious courtyard, the sun over the Santa Lucias warming my face. A large pepper tree scented the air. Gardens on all sides bloomed with varieties of California flowers in myriad colors. A bed of hundreds of white calla lilies bulged far into the yard, cutting off my slow circuit. Giant goldfish mesmerized children at the stone fountain in the center of the square. I sat on a low wall on the west side and let joy enfold me. Easter had really dawned two weeks early.

My mind turned gradually to the Gospel of the day, upon which I would soon be preaching. It was from John, chapter twelve:

> I solemnly assure you,
> unless the grain of wheat falls to the earth and dies,
> it remains just a grain of wheat.

161

But if it dies,
it produces much fruit.
The one who loves his life
loses it,
while the one who hates his life in this world
preserves it to life eternal.

What does it mean to "hate your life" as a Christian? Life is a gift from God. Why hate it? The key is love, not hate. It means to be so madly and passionately in love with God that all that matters is obeying and pleasing him. It is to be so in love with the Other that your own life ceases to be important. It is to give every inch, every ounce, and every minute of your life to God because you realize that it is all his gift of himself to you. It is to abandon yourself in total trust so that he becomes the root, the core, the "all in all" of your life. It is to hear God say, "Trust me," through thirty-one days and five hundred and fifty miles and never be hungry or unsheltered. It is not to try to figure life out yourself or grasp for yourself, but to let God be God and Lover and Giver *par excellence*. Yes, this Gospel is for lovers. When you can let your seed fall into the ground and die with Christ, then you can bear fruit. When you can let go of self-centeredness, when you can love so outrageously that only the Beloved is important, then you will understand what Jesus is about. The Christian vocation is the pilgrimage along the road toward that ideal. It is a slow and difficult process, but grace makes it possible.

That meditation became my homily, preached from the high pulpit with such animation that it took most of the Creed to regather my strength. My body knew that the Spirit had been at work.

Among the people who spoke to me after Mass, a heavy-set young woman politely suggested that I should not have acknowledged myself as the pilgrim in the homily. It would be better in the future to say, "I know a man who . . ." thus giving all the glory to God. Weighing that comment seriously, I concluded that it was better to "boast in the Lord" with St. Paul, as long as I strove to keep a pure heart. False modesty can weaken the challenge of the Gospel. I remember reading about an ancient monk who was tempted to forego a good work out of excessive humility. Catching himself, he addressed the tempter: "I did not begin this for your sake, Satan; so I'm not going to stop it for your sake, either."

Coffee and doughnuts were served after Mass. I struck up a conversation with the family that had brought the offertory gifts to the altar. They were Gene and Maureen and their two children, Anne, 16, and John, 10. Both parents were tall and good-looking. They seemed to be in their late thirties. After some chatter about pilgrimage, I commented on the excellent quality of liturgical music at the mission.

"We don't belong to the mission parish," Gene confessed a little sheepishly. "We overslept this morning and didn't want to go to our own parish and arrive late. We live in Toro Park, just this side of Salinas."

My mind clicked back, and then forward. I had passed Toro Park yesterday and would have to pass it again tomorrow on my way back through Salinas to get to Mission San Juan Bautista. Spontaneously I blurted, "Really? Would you be able to put me up tomorrow night?"

Without missing a beat Gene and Maureen agreed. The kids thought it a great idea. Dennis Hamm, who had arrived before Mass, just laughed and asked, "Is it always that easy?" I assured him it was not.

Dennis and I dined at a rather posh restaurant in Carmel. During the meal he asked, "What do you consider important learning moments or developments in your spiritual life that have come from the pilgrimage so far?" A typical Dennis question.

I counted several.

First, I thought I had gained some flexibility in surrendering to God's ways of leading me. The repeated admonition to trust was making it easier for me to let go and accept the Lord's providence.

Second, I felt that the meaning of humility was changing for me. Simplicity of heart was less elusive, being a natural outgrowth of my dependence on others for everything.

Next, I was observing a convergence between self-emptying and self-acceptance. As I experienced God's constant caring and affirmation, I was getting better at owning his love for me and accepting myself with greater conviction. Then emptying myself in imitation of Christ could change from unconscious self-rejection to intentional and fulfilling self-gift.

Finally, there was emerging within me a vaguely disturbing intuition that the pilgrimage would prove to be preparation for some trial or hardship I was going to undergo in the future. I did not have the foggiest notion what it would be, but I had a growing suspicion that I was being prepared for something which I would have to accept in total trust.

"If that's true," Dennis prophesied, "then whatever it is, it will be a call to mission . . . to service."

We lapsed into a pensive silence.

IV

"The Land Which I Promised"
Dt 34:4

Carmel to Berkeley
April 2–14, 1979

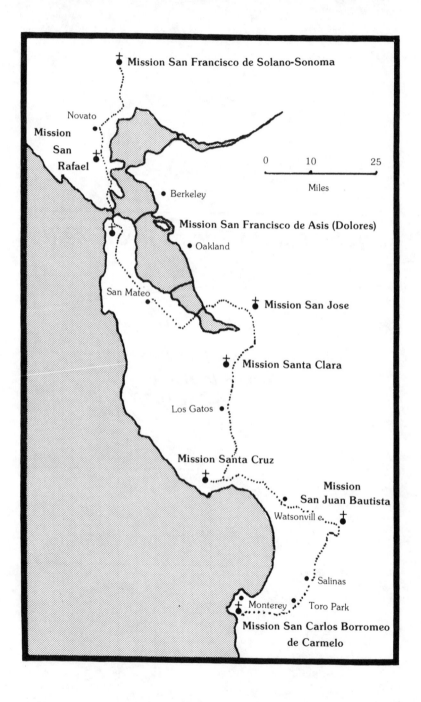

Mission San Francisco de Solano-Sonoma

Novato

Mission San Rafael

Berkeley

0   10   25

Miles

Mission San Francisco de Asis (Dolores)

Oakland

San Mateo

Mission San Jose

Mission Santa Clara

Los Gatos

Mission Santa Cruz

Mission San Juan Bautista

Watsonville

Salinas

Monterey   Toro Park

Mission San Carlos Borromeo de Carmelo

Monday, April 2.

Our problem is that we think we live between Easter and the parousia. We are restless like the Israelites between deliverance and the promised land. Unable to sustain enthusiasm after the exodus, they were soon murmuring against Moses and Yahweh for bringing them into the desert. For our part, we cannot long sustain our exhilaration over the resurrection, but are soon engulfed in the petty problems of daily life. If earthly joys are fragile, resurrection joy is chimerical.

Directors of the Ignatian Exercises frequently hear their retreatants say during the Fourth Week, "I cannot pray." Christ bursts from the tomb and the contemplations are powerfully consoling. A day or two later the retreatant is restless for the Exercises to be over, impatient to return to the activities of everyday life. There settles an ennui born of the conviction that one has gotten everything that the retreat has to offer. The problem is that the retreatant has not experienced the resurrection and the parousia converging and actualizing themselves in the present moment.

Like the Ignatian Fourth Week, this last segment of pilgrimage was both the easiest and the hardest. Carmel had been Easter. I had passed through purgation, passion and resurrection. I had been through bad weather, hard terrain, and physical pains. I had endured spiritual and emotional desolations. Now I was on the way home. Except for one day of mountains and another two of wind, the walking would be easy and through familiar territory. My legs were strong and my feet tough, except for the numbness. And begging was no longer very intimidating. Gone was the question of whether or not I could reach Sonoma. I had mapped out my route so that, barring unforeseen delay, I should arrive at the last mission on April 13, Good Friday. Challenge and uncertainty had all but disappeared.

The enemies from now on would be boredom and complacency. There is a principle in management which states that as a goal is approached, motivation wanes. I still wanted to get to Sonoma, and it was within reach. But that was not the primary purpose of the journey. What I was in danger of losing was the spirit, the enthusiasm, the union with Christ.

The eighteen miles to Toro Park were marked by boredom, frustration, sadness, and gratitude. I was bored and frustrated at having to backtrack a whole day to get to San Juan Bautista, up in the hills on the other side of Salinas. I was sad at leaving Carmel and grateful for all it had given me.

Having pre-arranged my lodging for this evening and having calculated that I could fairly easily reach Sonoma before Easter, I lapsed into a feeling of security and self-satisfaction.

A familiar voice inside me broke the silence: "Don't think the rest is all downhill, I can try your spirit as I have not yet. But you will be victorious. I am with you always, strengthening you with my grace."

"All right, Lord," I answered, "I'm as ready as I can ever be with your help. Just don't try me without preparing me."

Then he said something that shook my complacency: "I will take it away from you, so you don't get proud. You shall not finish. Like Moses, you shall see the promised land, but you shall not enter it. I will humble you."

I tried to protect myself by delivering a speech. It came out not as what I was feeling, but as what I imagined God wanted to hear: "All right, Lord. It's not my pilgrimage anyway. It's yours. Do as you please. You know my heart is set on finishing, but only if you will it and it is for your greater honor and service. I do not want to finish if it is to serve myself rather than you."

What had the voice meant by "You shall not finish"? And whose voice was it, the Lord's or mine? The Moses reference jarred me. He had died before entering the promised land. Was I willing to die? Almost before my mind had formulated the question, another voice spoke it: "Are you willing to die? What if 'not finish' means dying?"

Again I knew not whether it was his voice or mine, but a new kind of peace descended on me, and I heard myself answer as if the question had come from the Lord, "Yes, that's all right. As long as I know that that's what you want, I am willing."

I cannot say that I had never before contemplated and been reconciled to death. This was the first time, however, that it had happened in circumstances in which the possibility was real. As soon as I surrendered, the threat deflated. It was as if the Lord or my psyche immediately said, "Fine. Now that we've settled that, let's get on with the business of pilgriming." Obviously I did not die. The meaning of the encounter came clear only after I had returned to Berkeley.

Maureen, Gene, and their children welcomed me as sincerely as anyone had before. Maureen's dinner was prepared with care and skill. Conversation, which kept us at the table till 10:30, was lively and challenging. Yet within me was a growing sense of sameness. What was new to them was getting old to me. Even my gratitude for a roof and a bed was dulling. And in the morning, disengagement from my hosts would be another routine. I had learned something I did not want to learn: to protect my heart. I was becoming less vulnerable. Like my feet, my soul was being desensitized. Providence had become predictable.

Tuesday, April 3.

Mission San Juan Bautista lies in a valley beyond the hills northeast of Salinas. I arrived at 4:00 P.M. after a hot, boring, and lonely day.

The pastor received me with some embarrassment. Because he was having guests for the evening, he could not take me in. He proposed that I go to a Franciscan retreat house two miles away. After celebrating Mass alone in the cavernous old mission church, I found that the monsignor had changed his mind. He had remembered a room in a small annex behind the rectory. I would have to eat out, however. Tendering five dollars, the pastor suggested a nearby Mexican restaurant.

The least expensive combination on the menu, plus a glass of rosé and a modest tip, came to six dollars. Along the road I had found odd change totalling a little more than a dollar, so I was just able to cover it. I really wanted a second glass of wine, but if I had ordered it I would have had nothing for the waiter. My sense of justice got the better of me.

During the meal I was visited by a pervading sense of the Lord enfolding me, so compelling and pleasurable that I had to stop eating and surrender to it. It did not last long, subsiding as abruptly as it had come. Just a touch when I needed the assurance.

Wednesday, April 4.

After Mass and breakfast with the two sisters who worked at the mission, I set out on what would be another hot, boring day.

At about three o'clock I crossed the bridge into the south side of Watsonville. The main street was poor. With two quarters that the sisters had slipped into my lunch I bought a tall iced tea at the Woolworth's lunch counter, scant relief from the scorching sun.

I moseyed up to the north end of town and found a Catholic church, St. Patrick's. The interior was being painted, discouraging me from trying to pray there.

Having read my map incorrectly and thinking my route to Santa Cruz would take me out the south end of town, I doubled back to look for a place to stay. That was a mistake. South Watsonville is the Mexican enclave, comprised mostly of poor farm workers and their families. The language is Spanish. House after house I struggled to communicate. The scenario repeated itself with wives and mothers, old men and women, whoever was home.

"Do you speak English?" I would ask.

"No," would come the answer in Spanish.

"Well . . . uh . . . *yo* . . . (pointing to my chest) . . . uh . . . uh . . . pilgrim (making a walking movement with my fingers). *Yo* . . . uh . . . need . . . uh . . . FOOD (raising my voice as if volume would make up for the difference of language, and miming eating from a bowl with a spoon).

"Sí!" An amused nod. I thought I was making progress.

"And . . . uh . . . *yo* (apparently I knew only one word of Spanish) . . . uh . . . need . . . uh . . . a place to SLEEP (raising my voice again and resting my head sideways on my hands, palms together to form a pillow)."

"Sí!" Another amused nod.

"Can you take me in?"

"No hablo ingles." A helpless shrug.

"Gracias," I would mutter with resignation and an even more helpless shrug.

This went on and on. At a few houses I could get through in English. They were not interested in having me, though. One exchange offered momentary hope: "Come back when my husband gets home from work."

"When will that be?"

"Eleven."

"Thank you."

Toward the end I started showing the non-English speakers my California I.D. card. It had a picture of me in a Roman collar. Polite nods. No progress.

An intelligent-looking, well-dressed young man stood by a car in a driveway.

"Hi!" I started.

"Hi!" he answered. Here was my chance.

He listened intently to my whole story, nodding and smiling as I went along. When I finished, he listened for more. On a hunch, I asked, *"Hablas ingles?"* My Spanish was expanding.

"No ingles," came the answer, the smile unchanged.

I tramped off feeling like an idiot.

Still I did not want to give up. My pride kept me from falling back on a rectory. I crossed to the east side of the main street and decided to try a different neighborhood.

The first thing I encountered was a small playground with a green and white sign over the entrance: *Gift of the Chinese Benevolent Assn. of Watsonville.* There was also a row of Chinese characters which I presumed said the same thing.

"Wonderful!" I thought. "Now I'm going to have to speak Chinese!" The neighborhood was poor, with small houses set close together. I rang at the first door beyond the playground. A short, heavy-set young woman appeared with straight black shoulder-length hair parted in the middle. She wore a nightgown and a green bathrobe. She was Caucasian.

"Yes?"

And she spoke English!

"Hello. Is your husband home?" I preferred to speak with the husbands if they were there, to demonstrate that I was on the level.

"I don't have a husband."

"Oh, I see, Well, ny name is . . ."

I got as far as, " . . . usually stay at the missions, but when I'm between them I seek lodging from people along the way."

The woman cut me off with, "So you want a place to stay for the night? Sure. Come on in."

I had only made my speech as a formality, never thinking that a lone young woman would take me in. It was hard to keep surprise from registering on my face.

Joyce was thirty-six, though she looked only twenty-eight. She had a round, serious face with dark eyes, black eyebrows, and no makeup. She had lived in this single-story, two bedroom frame house all her life, and now that her only sister was married she lived here alone. Joyce was a self-proclaimed TV addict. The set was on all the time. There were no clocks in the house because Joyce told time by what was on the tube. She worked for the Registry of Motor Vehicles and attended the Catholic church on the other side of the bridge.

When I recounted my odyssey with the Mexicans, Joyce laughed and said, "You should have stayed up on the north side. They all speak English there, and they're better off."

Before long we were joined by Remie, the short, stocky, thirty-nine year old Japanese woman from next door who was Joyce's best friend. She had come for dinner.

Dinner was a sandwich. Joyce had bought an enormous bologna, cheese, and lettuce sandwich on a whole loaf of French bread. It had come in quarters, and Joyce had eaten one section for lunch. Each of us ate one of the three remaining quarters. Had I been as poor, would I have shared as freely? I wondered.

The three of us watched some game shows on TV and at about 8:15 I retreated to soak my feet before retiring. The numbness was moving across my soles, and I thought I could feel it starting up my right leg. It was beginning to frighten me. I would have to look for signs indicating whether the Lord wanted me to continue or quit the pilgrimage. I would be willing to stop if it became clear that that was his will. Sonoma was not worth permanent damage to my feet and legs. I remembered that St. Ignatius had harmed his own health by too vigorous penances in his early fervor. He later saw his folly and warned his men against similar errors. I would have to discern whether, in my own case, trust in God should take the shape of divinely inspired human prudence.

Thursday, April 5.

Voices from an old black-and-white movie slipped under my door from the television. It was 6:30. Joyce fixed a breakfast of eggs and toast, while I made a sandwich of lunch meats for the road. I really wanted to take two, having twenty miles to cover today, but I hesitated because Joyce had so little food in the house. Seeing me make only one, she said, "Santa Cruz is a long walk," and insisted that I take a second.

I was on the road at 7:45, the same time that Joyce left for work. The day was overcast and stayed that way. My route was a nondescript county road through Freedom, swinging around through Aptos and Soquel, north of Capitola, and into downtown Santa Cruz. The day was tedious and distracted. Joy had gone out of walking and praying and "being here" with the Lord. All I cared about was covering ground and "getting there." I was starting to count days. "After today, eight. After tomorrow, just a week." My only consolation was that I felt more assurance about my feet. Not that the numbness was subsiding. I just had an inner sense that the Lord wanted me to press forward and let him take care of them.

At three o'clock I stood facing Mission Santa Cruz. I entered without flourish. My interest in the missions was diminishing steadily. They were beginning to look all alike. The best ones were past, and the rest I could see by car from Berkeley. What was happening to me did not articulate itself. All I knew was that I felt unexplainably tired.

A half-size reproduction of the original mission church stands diagonally across a square from the massive neo-gothic church that now occupies the old site. I said a cursory prayer in the replica, then went to the rectory. A couple was at the door ahead of me talking to a woman in late middle age with gray hair. As the couple turned to leave, the woman inside moved to close the door. She may have thought I was one of the Santa Cruz street people, of whom there are many. I stepped forward quickly and identified myself, asking for one of the priests. She let me in.

A young, slender associate pastor with long brown hair and bushy brown beard listened to my story and showed me to a guest room. He was informal and brotherly, inviting me to concelebrate with him at 5:30 and preach about my journey.

Both priests at the mission were warm and hospitable, for which I was grateful. But this evening I ran short on enthusiasm. I had endured another tasteless day, and I was dreading the next day's hike over the Santa Cruz Mountains on Route 17. Narrow, winding, and with four lanes of fast traffic, it has been called the most dangerous stretch of highway in the United States. My misgivings stayed with me all evening and were aggravated by the weather. I awoke several times during the night to hear the clatter of rain.

Friday, April 6.

"Do you have a little time?" asked an attractive young woman after the 7:45 Mass. She wore her dark hair long, straight, and parted in the middle. Her face was dominated by wide, dark, cheerful eyes and large lips. Her trim figure sported a white blouse, blue jeans, and a plaid suit jacket. The total effect made her look nineteen or twenty. For her I could make time.

"Yes, I think so," I replied. Actually I had wanted to get an early start on my twenty miles over the mountains. My pack was ready for an immediate departure. At the last minute before Mass, the celebrant had asked me to preach again about pilgrimage, and now this woman wanted to hear more. We planted ourselves in one of the rectory parlors. Ordinarily I would not have lingered, but something told me she had more than pilgrimage on her mind.

Her name was Beth. She was twenty-five, a free lance writer, and a lover of all living things, especially plants. Sensitive and intelligent, she asked probing questions about my travels—writer's questions.

In time we got to talking about her, and a little bit of a miracle unfolded. Hers was a typical story. She had grown up in a working-class family with parents whose faith had been simple, authoritarian, and dogmatic. At the end of high school, she had rebelled against traditional values and had taken off with a couple of girl friends in a camper she had bought with her savings. They had gone in search of truth. Beth had a lot of resentment about the way the Catholic Church presented truth. She had once been severely disciplined in grade school for questioning something that a priest had said in his sermon, and she still felt the pain of it. She spoke of friends who had been psychologically injured by the Church's autocracy. Because of her upbringing, she had continued to "go to church" during the camper trip, but she was angry and questioning all the while. Finally she had found a priest in Banff, Canada who had told her what she wanted to hear: "Maybe you just aren't called to be a card-carrying member of the Roman Catholic Church." That had given her license to go her own way spiritually, which she did. It amused me, though, that she had needed a priest's permission to do it.

Beth had not received the sacraments in six years or even set foot inside a Catholic church in two. Then on this morning of Friday, April 6, 1979, she had awakened and started walking to a local breakfast shop, as was her custom. Her route, as usual, took her past Holy Cross Church, old Mission Santa Cruz. Looking at the spires as she had done many times in the past, she was affected in a way she had never been before. She had felt drawn magnetically across the square and into the church. She just happened to have gotten there fifteen minutes before a Mass was to begin. She had made the Stations of the Cross, and the confrontation with her religious heritage had brought her to tears. She just happened to have stayed for the Mass at which a young pilgrim Jesuit preached about total surrender to the promptings and providence of God, and she had been deeply touched. It had not been like the sermons she remembered from the past. Rather, it had been about passion and commitment and it had made sense to her for the first time. She had even felt drawn to receive the Eucharist, and in so doing had experienced an intimacy with Christ that was totally new to her.

Beth and I talked for an hour and a half. Several times I silently thanked God that the church had been locked when I had gone to celebrate a private Mass at 6:30.

After trading names and addresses, we walked down the hill together, she toward breakfast and I toward the mountains. I did not know what, if anything, would come of Beth's meeting with the Lord that morning. I did know, however, that she would not forget it and that she had admitted to herself and to me that it had been genuine. For starters, that was enough. In the words of Longfellow,

"Though the mills of God grind slowly, yet they grind exceeding small."

The Santa Cruz Mountains run northwest-southeast, separating the Monterey Bay/Salinas Valley area from the San Francisco Bay area. I bypassed the freeway out of Santa Cruz by taking Branciforte Drive, which twists gradually higher through impressive redwood forests, connecting with infamous Route 17 about half way to the summit. Thick dark clouds shrouded the mountains, several times dropping filmy drizzle so light and brief that it was not worthy of a poncho.

The next eight miles were hell. Walking conditions were by far the worst of the whole trip. I spent four hours picking my way along the edge of a four-lane highway without any bike or pedestrian lane. It swung around blind curves left and right, uphill and down. At times the distance between me and oncoming traffic was less than three feet. The flow was heavy, including eighteen-wheelers that threatened repeatedly to blow me away or suck me in. Sometimes, when there was no shoulder, I had to half-straddle an embankment to stay away from whizzing steel. Sometimes, if there were a guard rail, I could get outside it and step from head to head on the concrete pilings that shored up the mountainside. I did not say the beads, needing both hands to maneuver my staff. I just said Hail Marys over and over. Hundreds of them.

Coming down the north side was just as bad. Because it was downhill and because I was eager to get off this road, there was a tendency to go too fast and be careless. If my boot were to roll on loose gravel or eucalyptus nuts, I would be under rushing wheels.

Six or seven highway patrol cars cruised constantly. Because Route 17 was not a freeway, I was technically legal, so they did not stop me. One, however, slowed down and swerved toward me head on. Seeing me simply look up and nod, he drove off. Perhaps it was his way of chasing the idiot off the highway, or maybe he wanted to get a look at me to see if I were some kind of fugitive. I'll never know.

Finally, Route 17 straightened, widened, and planed off to a gradual descent. I had made it safely. It had to have been with God's help.

Lexington Reservoir lay ahead to the right, with St. Joseph's hill beyond it. Jesuit property. I had pretty much decided that after today's workout I would give myself a break and go to the former Jesuit novitiate in Los Gatos for the night. To test that proposition I begged at two houses on my left. At one of them the occupants were leaving for the weekend and at the other they were "plum full up." If I had a sleeping bag I was welcome to use the grounds, but no room in the house. So I headed for the old novitiate, which now is Sacred Heart Jesuit Center, a retirement community and the California Jesuit Provincial Headquarters.

One last obstacle confronted me. I had crossed to a breakdown lane on the right side of Route 17, where a high chain-link fence protected me from a steep, narrow ravine. That was fine for half a mile; then the breakdown lane disappeared. The highway had been built out over the ravine with no room between fence and traffic. On the far side the face of a cliff fell right down to the traffic lane, too. I was trapped.

Then the Lord provided again. A few feet behind me was a space under the fence just large enough to slide through. Lowering myself to the sheer embankment, I found that the next quarter-mile of highway rested atop I-beam pilings tall enough to allow a person to walk upright. Between the pilings was a footpath, which I followed. Traffic rolled quietly two feet above my head. Studying the dirt path, I recognized the familiar circular, waffle-iron bootprints that had faithfully accompanied me during the first two weeks. They were fresh and undisturbed. The last person to have walked this path before me had been that "guardian angel." Surfacing where the high-

179

way widened out again, I had no trouble the rest of the way. The incident reminded me of Alexander Pope. Forbidden to build a bridge across the highway that separated his home from his garden, Pope dug a tunnel, saying, "What we cannot overcome we must undergo."

I reached the Jesuit Center at 5:30, established my identity, and was welcomed into the community for the night.

One positive feature of the day's walk: it had not been boring.

Saturday, April 7.

Today was the easiest day of walking. It was almost like a fourth day of rest. The weather was sunny and warm; the road was straight and flat, through towns all the way; the distance was only ten miles; and the mission I was approaching stood on a Jesuit university campus, so I could anticipate ready hospitality.

Knowing how easy the day would be, I proceeded in a relaxed and carefree spirit, arriving at the University of Santa Clara in early afternoon. The administrator of the Jesuit community had no trouble giving me a room. I toured the campus, prayed in the mission church, and viewed the mission historical collection in the university art gallery.

In the evening I sat and talked with some of the Santa Clara Jesuits. They were curious about what I was doing, and very supportive. I think they were especially pleased that I was one of their own. It felt good to speak to my brother Jesuits about the experience of pilgriming. Prophets are frequently ignored in their own homes, and too often we religious fail to let the Lord speak to the members of our own communities through ourselves.

180

Sunday, April 8: Passion Sunday

After a concelebrated liturgy of the Lord's Passion in the mission church, I stopped to slip two palm fronds into the hollow top of my staff. As a freshman in high school I had read *Ivanhoe* and learned about the medieval "palmers," pilgrims returning to Europe after visiting the Holy Land. Palm branches attached to the tops of their staffs identified them as legitimate pilgrims and mendicants. Giving them food, alms, or hospitality would bring blessings on their benefactors. The palm symbol and the name "palmer" later came to denote any Christian pilgrim or sanctioned beggar. I suspect the surname Palmer is related. Anyhow, on this Palm Sunday I became a palmer heading home.

Departing for Mission San Jose a few minutes before ten, I almost collided with Theresa, a friend from Sacramento who was in town for a visit. She had graduated from Santa Clara a few years earlier. Scrutinizing me from head to toe, she gently poked at my ribs and complained, "Look how you've withered away to nothing!" She was right. I had started out at a hundred and forty-five pounds, and in five weeks had lost about twenty-five. My belt had shortened by four notches.

The walk between Mission Santa Clara and Mission San Jose would be only one day, and a short one at that: twelve miles. My route would take me through the north arm of San Jose, north through Milpitas, and into Fremont.

As diligently as I tried to live in the present and put everything in God's hands, I repeatedly found myself worrying about the future and trying to plan ahead. It was something like an insomniac straining at falling asleep. This time my concern was about Holy Thursday and Good Friday. I would probably miss the solemn liturgies if I were on the road. Projecting that I would be between San Rafael and Sonoma, I thought of having my own extended passion liturgy by staying outdoors Thursday night and keeping a vigil with Christ during his agony, arrest, and trials. During the next few days I would watch for confirmation of that plan from the Lord.

It was 3:30 when I arrived at Mission San Jose. The pastor would be out till six. Even the most leisurely tour of the mission could not be spread over two and a half hours. Believe me, I tried! It's even harder when it's your eighteenth mission in thirty-nine days. I inspected everything with greater attention than it deserved. Then I sat in the church to kill time. Not feeling at all in a mood for more prayer, I entertained myself by singing songs from the parish hymnal.

On my fourth trip back to the rectory, the pastor had arrived. He was a portly, black-haired man in his late forties. As soon as I explained that I was making a pilgrimage of the missions, we were buddies. He was an aficionado of mission history and had a soft spot for anyone who shared his interest.

I was to call him "Bill," and after he celebrated the 6:30 Mass we would go out to a Mexican restaurant, but not until he had made me one of his special margaritas. "Have you ever had a margarita? No? Good. Then your first one will be an excellent one. And how would you like to celebrate Mass tomorrow morning in the little chapel at the 'Ecce Homo' altar? Of course you would. And we can concelebrate. That will be wonderful!" He was irrepressible.

Before Mass Bill called the Dominican motherhouse behind the mission to see if the sisters could house me. The spare room in the rectory was occupied by a deacon working in the parish for a few months.

The margarita after Mass was an event in itself. Bill took a 1½ ounce shot-glass and started measuring out tequila into a blender. He counted aloud. When he got to five, I started to get nervous. He quit at seven. Mathematically that comes to more than five ounces per margarita. The walk to the car was a little unsteady.

It was after eleven when we left the restaurant, stuffed with Mexican food and mission stories. Unfortunately it was too late in the evening for such a meal. I awoke at 3:30 and enjoyed enchiladas till dawn.

Monday, April 9.

Today was a "first" and a "last." For the first and only time in the pilgrimage I hitchhiked. And for the last time I begged from door to door.

First the hitchhiking. I was on the east side of San Francisco Bay. To get to San Francisco I could walk back around the south end of the bay, losing a whole day, or I could cross one of the south bay bridges in a car. Pedestrian traffic is forbidden, except on the Golden Gate Bridge. Opting for the car, I walked the eight miles to the toll booth at the Dumbarton Bridge. A gale-force wind blasted against me off the bay, even worse than in the Salinas Valley. The last two miles were completely unnerving. I had to lean into the cold rush of air and push myself forward with my staff to make any progress at all. It was just before 1:00 when I reached the toll plaza.

I had made a sign of thick black marker on white typing paper: JUST ACROSS BRIDGE. One car went by while I was getting the sign out of my pack. I had to hold the paper against my chest to keep the wind from ripping it to shreds. A second car went by, the driver craning to catch my ad. The third vehicle, a brown pickup truck with a rack of auto windshields in the back, stopped. I had been there less than fifteen seconds. And I had been worried about losing time waiting for a ride!

I threw my staff into the back and my body into the cab. Naturally I was glad to have the ride, but I was even happier to be out of the wind. In the truck the air was warm and still, while outside the dirty brown bay was being churned furiously into whitecaps all around us.

The driver was a young black man named Leroy. Between his legs he held an open can of Miller, from which he occasionally slugged. He was inquisitive, so I told him about the pilgrimage. He understood it, however, as some kind of vacation and told me he preferred fishing.

Leroy let me off exactly where I had hoped he would, on Willow Road at U.S. 101. It was just 1:10, and I had twelve miles to go to reach San Mateo for the night.

The next few hours my spirits went rapidly downhill. While lunching I discovered that I had crossed the wrong bridge. If I had gone three extra miles to the San Mateo Bridge, it would have delivered me to the west side of the bay twelve miles farther north. My poor planning had cost me nine extra miles. I spent the next half hour kicking myself.

The farther north I walked, the stronger the wind blew against me. Prayer was impossible. I tried the rosary, but got nowhere. In the midst of this, I was getting more anxious about begging lodging in San Mateo. It was one thing to seek hospitality in wilderness or small towns. It would be quite another to do it in a suburb of San Francisco. I feared the suspicion and alienation that are endemic to big cities.

For two hours I raged against a headwind every bit as vicious as that of the Salinas Valley. It was a bitter reminder that these unnecessary miles were payment for my lack of foresight.

Needing a target for my anger, I railed against God until enough venom had spewed out to bring catharsis. The calm that followed brought shame, and the shame brought acceptance: "Thank you, Lord, for your power in the wind. Let it purify my heart. Let it blow away from me all that is not you. Just give me the strength to keep going." Once resigned, I could appreciate a mystery. My prayer of praise was the very labor of advancing, even if it seemed the antithesis of anything holy.

During the next hour I caught my first glimpse of San Francisco, clear and tiny across the water where the peninsula curved inward. It made the whole day worthwhile.

Shortly before five I crossed the line into San Mateo. I had had enough wind for one day, and it was time to look for hospitality. Ducking into the shelter of a side street, I found myself surrounded by low apartment buildings. A block ahead were some small, close-set private houses.

First house: no answer.

Second house: a young woman with long brown hair, fair complexion, small eyes, and glasses. She wore blue jeans and a print shirt. "I'll have to speak to my husband." Her voice sounded mellow and receptive. Leaving me outside, she disappeared.

Thirty seconds later a tall, bald man about forty came to the door. He had large, light eyes, fair skin, and a bushy, light-brown beard. What hair he had at the back of his head was light-brown, also, and flowed in long wisps down the back of his neck. He, too, wore jeans, and he was barefoot.

He studied me for about five seconds, then blurted gregariously, "Come on in!"

Mars and Louise were two of the most unconventional people I met during my wanderings. Mars, 40, had been a Catholic and had attended Catholic school through grade five. He had teenage children by a previous marriage. Louise, 32, had been raised Episcopalian. Now both were free spirits and were into Eastern religions, to the extent that their seven week old son was named after the Hindu god Arjuna. They were also into yoga, calisthenics, and natural foods. Both practiced professions: Louise as a seamstress and Mars as a card player. They were then in their second year of a two-year marriage contract, at the end of which, after a mandatory month of separation, they could renew or terminate. The contract was quite

185

detailed, specifying agreements each party made regarding issues that ranged from finances to pets. They had it typed on two sheets of floral paper and framed behind glass.

While Louise nursed Arjuna and shopped for our dinner, Mars and I talked about my pilgrimage and his religious views. "Prayer is not a lot of words asking for things," he asserted. "Prayer is what you do. Like being kind to people." Later he told me, "I'm into reincarnation. I think we're all incarnations of God." I pointed out that the Catholic doctrine is similar, but reversed. Rather than starting out as God, we are drawn into divinity through the grace of Christ. Mars expressed keen interest in my journey, especially my freedom, my communing with God in nature, and my relationships with people.

"You know why I let you in?" he asked. "We've had so-called 'Christians' come to the door before. They all wanted to 'do something' for Louise and me. They wanted to convert us. They never got in. And if I'd thought you were going to talk religion at me all night, you wouldn't have gotten in, either. I took you in because you were different. You hadn't come to 'save' me. Instead, you were in need. Instead of coming to do something for me, you came to let me do something for you. You put the whole deck into my hands and let me deal. You gave me all the power. That's different. That's why I let you in."

After an all-natural dinner of fresh chopped vegetables cooked in a wok, Louise and Mars and I talked far into the evening. Our easy rapport was something of a revelation to me. On the surface we were vastly different; in our hearts we were the same, each in our own way reaching for the Transcendent.

Tuesday, April 10.

With long farewells and bear-hugs, Mars and Louise turned me north on El Camino Real. This was a day I had

186

longed for. My eyes would close tonight in San Francisco. It was a city I had grown to love during the months before pilgrimage while working with the poor in the Tenderloin. It had signaled the beginning of Christwalk as my plane banked away toward San Diego. Now I was coming home. My vanity picked up, too. There was a nice ring to, "from San Diego to San Francisco."

As a day of pilgriming this one was a failure. My mind and heart were not at all with the Lord, and I was far from living in the present moment. The headwind was up again, and I was angry. When I wasn't cursing the wind, I was fearing begging in the Big City and plotting how to wriggle out of it. When I wasn't doing that, I was anticipating the glory of crossing the line from Daly City into San Francisco and devising suitable self-congratulations. It was all a regression which I attribute to the typical Fourth Week syndrome: getting tired of the already-but-not-yet between resurrection and homecoming.

In my distraction and haste I created a cramp in my left calf that stayed there almost the whole day.

The Lord's humor struck early in the afternoon when, thinking I was near the San Francisco border, I stopped to ask some workmen exactly where it lay. Pointing behind me, one of them said, "Back there a block or two." I had missed it. A dark cloud formed in my brain and rained on my pride. So much for glory.

My visit to Mission San Francisco de Asis, or Mission Dolores, as it is more commonly called, was hit-and-run—another result of my spiritual dryness. Out of a sense of obligation I took a quick turn through the museum and cemetery, having seen it all before. I celebrated a private Mass and within the hour was trotting toward the Jesuit campus of the University of San Francisco. My object was to (a) get as close to the Golden Gate Bridge as possible to shorten the next day's trek and (b) avoid begging. The Jesuit residence at U.S.F. was huge. Lots of rooms. Piece of cake.

187

"Did you write ahead?" inquired the Brother Guest-master, shuffling through his records. "We have a big convention in town. We're all full up."

After some dickering and explaining about pilgrimage and why I had not written, I was directed to Star of the Sea rectory on Geary, about fifteen blocks closer to the bridge. The pastor was a friend of the guestmaster.

In the space of my twenty minutes at U.S.F. the afternoon fog had rolled in. It was rain in suspension. Fifteen blocks later I looked as if I had come through a downpour.

The monsignor at Star of the Sea, a tall, slender, genteel and soft-spoken man in his fifties, met me in the parlor and listened politely.

"Would you be insulted if I asked for some identification?"

"Of course not." Thenceforth I was treated with curious admiration and utter graciousness.

Wednesday, April 11.

"Banana?" I asked.

"Yes. And the other one's chicken and butter."

Lots of butter. I had never heard of sandwiches like that before. But Maggie was hardly out of her teens and only five months out of Connemara. She was not yet familiar with American tastes. Also, she was probably still feeling her way around the rectory kitchen. I thanked her for making my lunch, bade the monsignor a grateful adieu, and turned west on Geary toward the Golden Gate Bridge.

Two weeks later I received a reflective letter from the monsignor. He told me that my pilgrimage reminded him of a verse called simply "Ode" by A.W.E. O'Shaughnessy, an Irish poet of the nineteenth century. He quoted the following lines:

We are the music-makers,
    And we are the dreamers of dreams,

Wandering by lone sea-breakers,
  And sitting by desolate streams;
World-losers and world forsakers,
  On whom the pale moon gleams:
Yet we are the movers and shakers
  Of the world for ever, it seems.

By ten o'clock I stood on the approach to The Bridge. My mind flashed back to the photograph on the wall of the Hungarians' kitchen in Del Mar. I remembered wondering if I would make it. It was the fulfillment of a dream. I *had* made it—after forty-two days and seven hundred and twenty miles.

The Bay area was clear, with good visibility in all directions: the city, Marin County, the Berkeley campanile, Oakland, Richmond, the Pacific. They were all there, and I felt they were all mine. Joggers and cyclists and roller skaters went by. Tourists gaped. An oriental woman asked me to snap her picture with one of the suspension towers in the background. The breeze off the ocean exhilarated me, and I felt like running up to people and saying, "Do you know how far I've walked to cross this bridge today?" I restrained myself.

On the Marin side, I got down to the business of choosing a route to San Rafael. My map showed several possibilities, so I decided to ask directions to get the straightest shot. At the north end of Sausalito I tried a combination bait shop and gin joint. At the bar were three under-employed fishermen and a half-drunk middle-aged woman with two beers in front of her. They got into a free-for-all over which would be my best route. The tracks were straightest, but the tunnels were blocked. The road was too roundabout. Finally piecing together their conflicting stories, I decided to follow the tracks as far as the high school, then switch to the road over the grade into Corte Madera, through Larkspur, over the Wolfe Grade, and into San Rafael. With a couple more checks on my directions along the way, I made it to Mission San Rafael at 3:00 P.M.

Hospitality was guaranteed. One of the resident priests was the Catholic chaplain at San Quentin, where I had worked as a tertian. I was welcomed as an old friend.

During the day I had imperceptibly entered a spiritual limbo. Content with having reached the Golden Gate, I viewed the home-stretch as anticlimactic, an exercise in perseverance to say I had gone the whole route. That attitude contaminated my deeper soul, suggesting that the time of significant growth was over. My heart had already begun to say goodbye to the pilgrim's spontaneous trust.

In that mode my thoughts skipped to the solemn triduum of Holy Week. Ideas were forming around how I wanted the pilgrimage to end. Tomorrow I would go ten miles north to Novato, request lodging at the rectory, and concelebrate at the Mass of the Lord's Supper. Having abandoned the idea of an outdoor walking vigil throughout Holy Thursday night, I was considering a night of contemplation in the church at Novato. On Good Friday I would try to reach Sonoma in time for the Liturgy of the Passion, after which I could touch down at the last mission. One of the tertians would drive me back to Berkeley and my travels would be over. It was all very neat in my mind.

The first sign that the Lord had different plans was when the pastor at San Rafael called the pastor at Novato and learned that his rectory was full. Tomorrow would be more interesting than I desired.

April 12. Holy Thursday

The next-to-last day. Firsts and lasts have intrinsic dignity. Seconds and next-to-lasts are contingent, anticlimactic, often marked by anxiety or letdown. That was Holy

Thursday, a hodge-podge of worry and distrust. Where would I stay in Novato? Would I miss the Liturgy of the Lord's Supper? How would I pay the admission at the Sonoma mission, a state historical site? Would the numbness of my feet prove a symptom of some permanent damage? Should I have quit when the toes first began to lose sensation? Would I need a more detailed map so as not to go astray on the last day?

The short jaunt from San Rafael to Novato was an uninterrupted parade of these petty, self-centered concerns, the worst of which was a detailed, angry fantasy about the pastor's refusal to offer me hospitality. I had regressed to a pre-pilgrimage state, surrendering to my passion for security and certitude. Two dynamics seem to have become operative. First I was grieving over the imminent end of my journey, the return to ordinary life, and the forfeiture of opportunities and challenges that a longer road might offer. Second, I was reacting to a parasitic fear that the entire project would prove futile because I had not been dramatically and permanently changed. Knowing myself to be the same Dick Roos who had set out six weeks earlier, I was metaphorically throwing up my hands in defeat, reclaiming control of my life, and, in effect, quitting the pilgrimage before it was over.

Midday found me in Novato on the steps of the little house that served as the parish rectory. It was a mile from the church. There was indeed no room for me there, but the pastor had arranged lodging for me near the church at the home of the sexton. Once again my worry and anger had been unwarranted.

The sexton, a quiet man in his fifties who had retired early from a business career, was named Everett. Everyone, however, called him Woody, nicked from his middle name, Woodrow Wilson. Besides caring for the church Woody dabbled in oil painting and served as the family cook. Woody's wife, a diminutive woman with impaired hearing, held the post of parish organist.

The couple had two daughters: Denise, a thin, quiet seventeen-year-old whose passions included knick-knacks, television, and chocolate; and an older girl, twenty-four, who no longer lived at home. Two dogs enjoyed positions as almost equal members of the family.

Woody and his wife were simple, pious people, formed in the attitude that priests are a breed above and apart. They treated me with such deference and solicitude that their efforts at making me comfortable had the opposite effect.

I phoned Berkeley and arranged for Dennis Hamm to pick me up at the Sonoma Mission between 4:00 and 5:00 the following afternoon. Then I called St. Francis Solano Parish in Sonoma to find out what time their Good Friday liturgy was scheduled to start. I was irked to learn that they retained the pre-Vatican II practice of observing the passion from twelve till three. If I wanted to attend, I would have to walk twenty miles by noon.

My obsession with the Holy Week liturgies was rooted in my feeling disenfranchised. I am a priest for whom prayerful and engaging liturgy is paramount, yet here I was without a community to minister to, or even belong to, at the most solemn time of the Church year. To compensate I had inflated my expectations of the Sacred Triduum liturgies such as could only lead to disappointment.

That evening the Mass of the Lord's Supper was indeed a letdown, performed in perfunctory style with no foot-washing and hardly any congregational singing. My sadness deepened when, back home, Woody's wife said to me, "You're probably wondering, Father, why we didn't receive Communion. It's because we went to Mass this morning and received then." If the parish organist and sexton were deprived of the Eucharist at the solemn commemoration of the Last Supper simply because they lacked up-to-date instruction, how many others suffered the same injustice? And why were they left uninformed? We are a Church of sinners—in the pulpits as well as the pews.

April 13. Good Friday

At six the sun rose on a clear, warm day. I was already walking, my head full of distractions about reaching Sonoma by noon, achieving the coveted goal, and returning in triumph to Berkeley. Though the country road was peaceful and conducive to meditation, I was too excited to focus. As the morning wore on, my Good Friday fast began to take effect, hunger becoming participation in the passion. Toward noon I was feeling hot, weak, and woozy.

Suddenly adrenalin shot through me. Dead ahead, at the end of a straight stretch of Route 12, stood what I knew to be the Sonoma City Hall. The mission would be a block to the right. This was the last mile. To prepare myself I took a long drink at a nearby gas station, hitched my straw hat to my pack, washed my face and hands, and combed my hair. One would have thought the media were waiting.

It ended "not with a bang, but a whimper." That interminable mile deposited me in the small reconstruction of the chapel of San Francisco de Solano. Since the state had taken it over as an historical monument, the Eucharist was not reserved there. The chapel was just an interesting room. Nevertheless it had been my goal for forty-four days and almost eight hundred miles. As a gesture of thanksgiving I kissed the tiled floor before the main altar. It was a dry formality, because I felt nothing. I had intended to say, with Christ at the end of his hours on the cross, "It is finished." The words never entered my mind. Instead I heard questions to which I had no answers: "So what? Why did you bother? What was it all worth, anyway?"

I dragged myself glumly to the parish church a few blocks away and endured an overcrowded service that seemed as disjointed and drawn out as the passion it memorialized.

Nothing was as it should have been. No joy of completeness. No satisfaction. I was too deflated even to be angry. Yet I did not know why. Eventually, while waiting for Dennis back at the mission, I remembered the Lord's admonition of a few days earlier: "I can still take it away from you." He had. In the past two days I had taken charge of the pilgrimage, having decided how I wanted it to end. Now he was showing me that that was merely self-defeating.

My reception home was subdued, with only three members of the community present. After a simple meal, I just wanted to sleep, but that was not to be. One of our tertians was to preside at the theology school's Passion Liturgy at 8:00 P.M. and my presence would mean a lot to him. Still depressed, and unable to muster the energy to shower and change, I attended in my pilgrim garb. That proved to be symbolic. Christwalk was not yet over.

April 14. Holy Saturday

At 5:30 I was awake and ready to walk, with no place to go. Something in me still felt a need to press forward. As at Carmel, I was reliving the dazed disconnectedness between death and resurrection. I stepped out of bed and into a web of trivia that held me the whole day: six weeks of mail; laundry; anecdotal conversations; shopping for frozen pizza for dinner. Little things. Nothing of moment.

My postpartum depression hung on, pushing my psyche back out on the road. If what I had done was incomplete and futile, what must I do to give it wholeness and meaning? There must be more.

While this was going on, I was noticing changes in myself. For example, I could not put on my wristwatch. It signified a form of slavery to time, a manacle. I have not worn one since.

My sense of speed and distance had shrunk. Driving a car for the first time, I found myself repeatedly braking to a crawl. Acceleration beyond a walking pace seemed unnatural, as did distances beyond twenty-five miles. The prospect of driving a hundred miles and returning in the same day seemed surreal. Flying to Los Angeles in an hour was unthinkable.

Proprietorship became a wholly new experience. Throughout the day I would glance across at my bed, almost disbelieving that it would be there for me that night and every night. My puttering was punctuated by regular trips to the refrigerator. I would peruse what was there and decide I was not really hungry. What had drawn me was not a desire to eat, but a need to see the food and know that I did not have to ask anyone for it. It was mine. No more begging. The same was true of money. The pizza run was my first occasion to use cash I had not begged or received as a gift. It had come from the tertianship treasury and I had a right to use it. Though small in amount, it symbolized power and independence. I was no longer disenfranchised. Though it made me feel liberated and secure, I knew with a certain sadness that before long I would again be taking food and money for granted. It would be, regrettably, the loss of regained innocence.

Day flowed into evening, and evening flowed into the Easter Vigil. Dressing up in a suit and tie gave me a feeling of purpose, so I resolved to escape my doldrums and enter into the spirit of the feast.

The liturgy began with a procession of eight performers: a singer, a poet, two white-face mimes, a dancer, and several others. The deacon carried an oversized resurrection candle and set it to one side of the sanctuary, with the troupe gathered around it.

"These are the pilgrims," announced the celebrant. My throat tightened and my heart began to race. The theme of the whole celebration was pilgrimage, and each segment represented an evening story told around the pilgrims' campfire, the candle. The readings were delivered in a variety of media: creation was mimed, deliverance was sung, another mystery was danced, a fourth was in poetry, and so on. Each "story" ended with the entire congregation rising, lifting our arms to the sky, and being led in a prayer about our shared pilgrimage to the Father. I could feel life returning.

The homily touched so closely on my experience of the previous six weeks that I felt certain the Lord was directing it at me. With the preacher's permission I quote the following section:

> We have come here this evening as a pilgrim people, a people on a journey, a people who have paused for a while to listen to stories, revelations of God's utter faithfulness. And God *is* faithful. . . .
>
> . . . God is so faithful, he has gone down with us into the very marrow of our existence and he has brought us home, freed us yet again from betrayal, denial, cowardice. . . .
>
> . . . God is so faithful, he has wooed and caressed us when we felt forsaken, abandoned, entirely alone, "as cold as last year's love."
>
> God is so faithful, he has cooled us and given us refreshment, refreshment from the sometimes relentless aridity of our lives. . . .

The seventh "evening story" of the pilgrimage was the Eucharistic meal. After Communion with the resurrected Lord we all stood and raised our arms for the final prayer, but I did not hear it. Something inside flipped over and slid into place, and I knew I had arrived. Unable to contain myself, I whispered through my tears, "It is finished."

It was right for Christwalk to end in the resurrection, but death had to come first. I had to see the broken pieces of my way lying on the ground, and I had to let the Master pick them up and put them together his way.

As the congregation began the recessional, I heard once more the Lord's familiar words: "Trust me. Just trust me." And then a voice of my own: "I'm home. I have come home."

Epilogue

"Come and See"
Jn 1:39

When John the Baptizer sent his disciples over to Jesus, they asked their new leader where he made his home. Rather than naming a place, the Lord replied, "Come and see." Jesus' home is not a place, but a mission; and the heart at rest in Jesus, wherever he leads, is at home.

People have asked how my six weeks on the road changed me. I used to concoct elaborate theories about that, as if the pilgrimage would be a failure if I had not been radically transformed. Five years later I am at peace with the admission that my Christwalk was a watershed experience of the goodness of God and people that did not change me, but rather afforded continuing growth through reflective discovery. I have noticed in these last years that my definition of prayer has broadened to include any creative activity that manifests God in the world. I am more attuned to God's action in the ordinary events of life and am more ready to let God define the circumstances in which he will reveal himself, rather than limiting God by my own preconceptions. Finally, in the last five years I have had to make several choices regarding mission and ministry. In so doing I have noticed in myself clearer trust in responding to God's calls and less reliance on natural reason alone. One could justifiably call the pilgrimage a turning point in my life, but there have been many, and I am still the same person—dynamic, not static. Life is pilgrimage, and mine is still going on.

Would I do it again? What would I do differently? Would I recommend it to others? These are questions I hear frequently. Yes, I would do it again, but only if I were convinced the Lord was calling me. So far I have no evidence of that.

If I went out again I would go slower, not pressing toward a goal. I would stay with people longer and get to know them better, entering more deeply into their struggles and their faith-lives. In recent years I have outgrown much of my fear of being ordinary, so my starting point would be very different. "He saved others; let him save himself," they said of the crucified one. He did not need to save himself. He was free to let God do it. I believe I have moved a pace or two toward that freedom.

If I were to set out again I would not march so relentlessly as to numb my feet. They did recover, by the way. Two months after Easter feeling was back to normal. Though foolhardy, it taught me something about my need to succeed.

As for recommending pilgrimage to others, yes, I would. But not for everyone. If I were a director of religious formation, I would restrict pilgrimage to more mature members who had discerned and were convinced it was an invitation from God. That was what made it possible for me, and at times it was the only thing that kept me going.

Pilgrimage can be an effective witness against the isolation and alienation that characterize society today. People who met and hosted me found that it *is* possible to trust a stranger and be enriched by the encounter. Our world needs that. The sobering alternative was voiced by a Jesuit in Berkeley less than a week after my return: "In today's society the burden of credibility rests on the pilgrim. There's too much crime in the world for people to feel conscience-bound to open their homes to a stranger. What if someone is killed someday because, having trusted you, they trust the next stranger who comes to their door?"

That is both possible and frightening, yet Christianity still calls us to risk. Alienation and violence are part of the world, the social effects of sin. If we Christians do nothing to shift the balance, we are admitting that Jesus died in vain.

Of all the apostles of healing and hope, one of the most inspiring has been Fr. Pedro Arrupe, Superior General Emeritus of the Society of Jesus. For eighteen years he led the Church's largest religious order through the desert of post-Vatican II reform and renewal, his own body ravaged for the last two by an incapacitating stroke. On September 3, 1983, in a final address to the delegates gathered in Rome to elect his successor, the text of which had to be read by an assistant because of Father Arrupe's inability to speak, the holy man used words which, for me, express acutely the omega point of the human pilgrimage:

"Now, more than ever, I find myself in the hands of God. This is what I have wanted all my life, even from my youth. And this is still the one thing I want. But now there is a difference: the initiative is entirely with God."[10]

Notes

1. Translated by R.M. French. New York, Ballantine, 1974.

2. Scripture quotes are from the New American Bible, unless otherwise noted at the end of the quote.

3. Rome, E.J. Dwyer, 1978; Garden City, N.Y., Doubleday, 1980.

4. *Be Not Afraid* by Robert J. Dufford, S.J. Copyright © 1975 by Robert J. Dufford, S.J. and North American Liturgy Resources, 10802 North 23rd Avenue, Phoenix, Arizona 85029. All rights reserved. Used with permission.

5. *Only in God* by John B. Foley, S.J. Copyright © 1976 by John B. Foley, S.J. and North American Liturgy Resources, 10802 North 23rd Avenue, Phoenix, Arizona 85029. All rights reserved. Used with permission.

6. Copyright 1968 by World Library Publications of G.I.A. Publications, Inc., Chicago, Ill. 60638. All rights reserved. Used with permission.

7. New York, Macmillan, 1970.

8. Peter Shaffer, Avon Paperbacks, 1977.

9. *The Grapes of Wrath,* Penguin Paperbacks, 1977.

10. *Documents of the 33rd General Congregation of the Society of Jesus,* The Institute of Jesuit Sources, Saint Louis, Mo., 1984, p. 93.